Cryptocurrencies

A Profound Introduction For Beginners

Johan Von Amsterdam

Cryptocurrencies

© Copyright All rights reserved.

This document is geared towards providing exact and reliable information in regards to the topic and issue covered. The publication is sold with the idea that the publisher is not required to render accounting, officially permitted, or otherwise, qualified services. If advice is necessary, legal or professional, a practiced individual in the profession should be ordered.

- From a Declaration of Principles which was accepted and approved equally by a Committee of the American Bar Association and a Committee of Publishers and Associations.

In no way is it legal to reproduce, duplicate, or transmit any part of this document in either electronic means or in printed format. Recording of this publication is strictly prohibited and any storage of this document is not allowed unless with written permission from the publisher. All rights reserved.

The information provided herein is stated to be truthful and consistent, in that any liability, in terms of inattention or otherwise, by any usage or abuse of any policies, processes, or directions contained within is the solitary and utter responsibility of the recipient reader. Under no circumstances will any legal responsibility or blame be held against the publisher for any reparation, damages, or monetary loss due to the information herein, either directly or indirectly.

Respective authors own all copyrights not held by the publisher.

The information herein is offered for informational purposes solely, and is universal as so. The presentation of the information is without contract or any type of guarantee assurance.

The trademarks that are used are without any consent, and the publication of the trademark is without permission or backing by the trademark owner. All trademarks and brands within this book are for clarifying purposes only and are the owned by the owners themselves, not affiliated with this document.

JOHAN VON AMSTERDAM
A gift as a thank you!

The cryptocurrency world is a fast moving world.

If you want to stay up-to-date, please check out the author's website:

http://www.aboutcryptocurrencies.net

Here you will find the latest cryptocurrencies news gathered from around the world and updated multiple times per day.

Sign-up for the 'Daily Crypto News' and receive the electronic version of one of the officially published books for free as a thank you for buying this book.

- So go to http://www.aboutcryptocurrencies.net
- sign up
- get the 'Bitcoin: What is Bitcoin?' as a thank you.

Don't forget, only make educated decisions!

Yours sincerely,

Johan von Amsterdam

Table of Contents

PART 1: WHAT IS BITCOIN — 8

CRYPTOCURRENCY: THE FUTURE OF FINANCIAL TRANSACTIONS — 9

INTRODUCTION TO BLOCKCHAIN — 11

WHY BITCOIN? — 17

OTHER CHARACTERISTICS OF BITCOIN — 20

WHAT IS A BITCOIN WALLET? — 22

HOW TO CREATE A BITCOIN WALLET — 25

GETTING YOUR FIRST FREE BITCOINS — 30

BUYING BITCOIN HAND-TO-HAND — 32

BITCOIN INVESTMENT STRATEGY — 37

BITCOIN VOLATILITY — 40

TIPS FOR NEW BITCOIN TRADERS — 44

CONCLUSION — 47

PART 2: BITCOIN CASH VERSUS BITCOIN — 50

INTRODUCTION	52
INTRODUCTION TO CRYPTOCURRENCIES	53
THE BASICS OF BITCOIN	56
BITCOIN PROTOCOLS	61
BITCOIN PRIVATE KEYS	67
BETWEEN A HARD AND A SOFT FORK!	71
BTC VERSUS BCH	77
THE SPLIT!	81
AFTERMATH OF THE BITCOIN SPLIT	85
PART 3: MONERO VERSUS BITCOIN	**88**
INTRODUCTION	90
REAL WORLD EXAMPLES	93
BITCOIN	105
MONERO	115
THE BATTLE OF THE CRYPTOCURRENCIES	123

HOW TO BUY?	128
STORING CRYPTOCURRENCIES	130
EPILOGUE PART 3	142
PART 4: RIPPLE VS BITCOIN	**143**
BITCOIN VS. RIPPLE: AN INTRODUCTION	145
BITCOIN	148
RIPPLE	157
REAL WORLD EXAMPLES	164
HOW TO BUY BITCOIN AND RIPPLE	173
HOW TO STORE	179
BEFORE INVESTING	182
WHO IS THE WINNER, BITCOIN OR RIPPLE?	200
THANK YOU!	202

Part 1: What is Bitcoin

Unlock the Mystery of Bitcoin

- Do you want to know what is the best and safest exchange to buy your Bitcoin?

- Do you want to know where and how to store your new investment safely?

Then start reading this part of the book.

In this informative, must-have guide, you will discover all you need to know about Bitcoin, including how to set up your wallet, the best apps for mobile devices, and how to buy your first bitcoins.

We will start from the beginning, learning about Bitcoin history and the numerous advantages Bitcoin investing has over government-controlled money. We will teach you how to protect your Bitcoin investments, introducing you to the block chain technology and the smart contracts principle.

After reading this part of the book you will be able to:

- Build Your Own Web Wallet

- Know How to Buy Bitcoins

- Acquire Bitcoins for Free

- Decide Where to Keep Your Bitcoins

- Develop Strategies for Protecting Your Bitcoin Investments

- Understand Different Investment Strategies

Cryptocurrency: The Future of Financial Transactions

If you are asked what the birth of cryptocurrency, would bring to the world of finance, the first thing that will probably cross your mind is what is cryptocurrency? This thought however, will only come to the mind of people who are not well versed with the existing online currencies. But, if you are one of the few but dominant figures who know cryptocurrencies even if your eyes are closed, you would be able to answer the question more elaborately.

So to speak, the actual start of the turmoil existed when Bitcoin was introduced to the world and eventually became the most famous and wanted cryptocurrency. This project was started primarily to answer the lingering complains of people whose money and assets are held by one centralized unit (and often intervened by the government itself) and whose transfers are limited and frozen at a timely basis. With the start of Bitcoin, many had the option to acquire an online coin or currency that they can use similarly with fiat money. Although acquiring it is tedious and requires resources, many were attracted to it from the very start because many were wanting to break away with the confinement of a single entity controlling everything else in terms of finance.

Slowly, Bitcoin started to gain actual monetary value and new types of cryptocurrencies came into existence as a possible answer to the problems that Bitcoin imposes and also to create their own currencies that people can opt to use as the one generated from the former is limited and hard to acquire.

Although cryptocurrency was not widely accepted, it slowly gained its momentum and now, many other businesses even accept it as a form of payment or exchange. The very same thing is slowly happening to new crypto currencies. Although the profits are not guaranteed and the software running them is open-source, many still try to vie to acquire these currencies as another means of investment.

If this kind of merge between technology and finance continues to improve over time, it will be no wonder if more and more people will divert their attention to acquiring these coins and more businesses will open themselves to exchanging and accepting them as actual reward or trade for good and services. Like everything else, the slow but steady approach of crypto currency could result to major changes in the way finance has been seen and treated in the past.

More people are opening their minds to the existence and stability of such platforms and many are craving to break away from the scrutinizing eyes of the governing bodies involved in the storage and exchange of their assets. The future may seem dim this day but as more creative minds work together to make more convenience in the way finance and everything monetary is treated. Who knows maybe one day even fiat money can disappear for good.

The question that remains now would be if the government will allow such major changes that will incur their lost or will such things also change the way our government runs and thinks.

Introduction to Blockchain

If you've attempted to dive into this mysterious thing called blockchain, you will be forgiven for recoiling in horror at the sheer opaqueness of the technical jargon that is often used to frame it. So before we get into what a Bitcoin is we need to know how blockchain technology might change the world, let's discuss what blockchain actually is.

In the simplest terms, a blockchain is a digital ledger of transactions, not unlike the ledgers we have been using for hundreds of years to record sales and purchases. The function of this digital ledger is, in fact, pretty much identical to a traditional ledger in that it records debits and credits between people. That is the core concept behind blockchain; the difference is who holds the ledger and who verifies the transactions.

With traditional transactions, a payment from one person to another involves some kind of intermediary to facilitate the transaction. Let's say Rob wants to transfer $20 to Melanie. He can either give her cash in the form of a $20 note, or he can use some kind of banking app to transfer the money directly to her bank account. In both cases, a bank is the intermediary verifying the transaction: Rob's funds are verified when he takes the money out of a cash machine, or they are verified by the app when he makes the digital transfer. The bank decides if the transaction should go ahead. The bank also holds the record of all transactions made by Rob, and is solely responsible for updating it whenever Rob pays someone or receives money into his account. In other words, the bank holds and controls the ledger, and everything flows through the bank.

That is a lot of responsibility, so it's important that Rob feels he can trust his bank otherwise he would not risk his money with them. He needs to feel confident that the bank will not defraud him, will not lose his money, and will not be robbed and will not disappear overnight. This need for trust has underpinned pretty much every major behaviour and facet of the monolithic finance industry, to the extent that even when it was discovered that banks were being irresponsible with our money during the financial crisis of 2008, the government (another intermediary) chose to bail them out rather than risk destroying the final fragments of trust by letting them collapse.

Blockchains operate differently in one key respect: they are entirely decentralised. There is no central clearing house like a bank, and there is no central ledger held by one entity. Instead, the ledger is distributed across a vast network of computers, called nodes, each of which holds a copy of the entire ledger on their respective hard drives. These nodes are connected to one another via a piece of software called a peer-to-peer (P2P) client, which synchronises data across the network of nodes and makes sure that everybody has the same version of the ledger at any given point in time.

When a new transaction is entered into a blockchain, it is first encrypted using state-of-the-art cryptographic technology. Once encrypted, the transaction is converted to something called a block, which is the term used for an encrypted group of new transactions. That block is then sent (or broadcast) into the network of computer nodes, where it is verified by the nodes and, once verified, passed on through the network so that the block can be added to the end of the ledger on everybody's computer, under the list of all previous blocks. This is called the chain, hence the tech is referred to as a blockchain.

Once approved and recorded into the ledger, the transaction can be completed. This is how cryptocurrencies like Bitcoin work.

Accountability and the removal of trust

What are the advantages of this system over a banking or central clearing system? Why would Rob use Bitcoin instead of normal currency?

The answer is trust. As mentioned before, with the banking system it is critical that Rob trusts his bank to protect his money and handle it properly. To ensure this happens, enormous regulatory systems exist to verify the actions of the banks and ensure they are fit for purpose. Governments then regulate the regulators, creating a sort of tiered system of checks whose sole purpose is to help prevent mistakes and bad behaviour. In other words, organisations like the Financial Services Authority exist precisely because banks can't be trusted on their own. And banks frequently make mistakes and misbehave, as we have seen too many times. When you have a single source of authority, power tends to get abused or misused. The trust relationship between people and banks is awkward and precarious: we don't really trust them but we don't feel there is much alternative.

Blockchain systems, on the other hand, don't need you to trust them at all. All transactions (or blocks) in a blockchain are verified by the nodes in the network before being added to the ledger, which means there is no single point of failure and no single approval channel. If a hacker wanted to successfully tamper with the ledger on a blockchain, they would have to simultaneously hack millions of computers, which is almost impossible. A hacker would also be pretty much unable to bring a blockchain network down, as, again, they would need to be able to shut down every single computer in a network of computers distributed around the world.

The encryption process itself is also a key factor. Blockchains like the Bitcoin one use deliberately difficult processes for their verification procedure. In the case of Bitcoin, blocks are verified by nodes performing a deliberately processor- and time-intensive series of calculations, often in the form of puzzles or complex mathematical problems, which mean that verification is neither instant nor accessible. Nodes that do commit the resource to verification of blocks are rewarded with a transaction fee and a bounty of newly minted Bitcoins. This has the function of both incentivising people to become nodes (because processing blocks like this requires pretty powerful computers and a lot of electricity), whilst also handling the process of generating - or minting - units of the currency. This is referred to as mining, because it involves a considerable amount of effort (by a computer, in this case) to produce a new commodity. It also means that transactions are verified by the most independent way possible, more independent than a government-regulated organisation like the FSA.

This decentralised, democratic and highly secure nature of blockchains means that they can function without the need for regulation (they are self-regulating), government or other opaque intermediary.

Let the significance of that sink in for a while and the excitement around blockchain starts to make sense.

Smart contracts

Where things get really interesting is the applications of blockchain beyond cryptocurrencies like Bitcoin. Given that one of the underlying principles of the blockchain system is the secure, independent verification of a transaction, it's easy to imagine other ways in which this type of process can be valuable. Unsurprisingly, many such applications are already in use or development.Some of the best ones are:

Smart contracts (Ethereum): probably the most exciting blockchain development after Bitcoin, smart contracts are blocks that contain code that must be executed in order for the contract to be fulfilled. The code can be anything, as long as a computer can execute it, but in simple terms it means that you can use blockchain technology (with its independent verification, trustless architecture and security) to create a kind of escrow system for any kind of transaction. As an example, if you're a web designer you could create a contract that verifies if a new client's website is launched or not, and then automatically release the funds to you once it is. No more chasing or invoicing. Smart contracts are also being used to prove ownership of an asset such as property or art. The potential for reducing fraud with this approach is enormous.

Cloud storage: cloud computing has revolutionised the web and brought about the advent of Big Data which has, in turn, kick started the new AI revolution. However, most cloud-based systems are run on servers stored in single-location server farms, owned by a single entity (Amazon, Rackspace, Google etc). This presents all the same problems as the banking system, in that you data is controlled by a single, opaque organisation which represents a single point of failure. Distributing data on a blockchain removes the trust issue entirely and also promises to increase reliability as it is so much harder to take a blockchain network down.

Digital identification: two of the biggest issues of our time are identify theft and data protection. With vast centralised services such as Facebook holding so much data about us, and efforts by various developed-world governments to store digital information about their citizens in a central database, the potential for abuse of our personal data is terrifying. Blockchain technology offers a potential solution to this by wrapping your key data up into an encrypted block that can be verified by the blockchain network whenever you need to prove your identity. The applications of this range from the obvious replacement of passports and I.D. cards to other areas such as replacing passwords. It could be huge.

Digital voting: highly topical in the wake of the investigation into Russia's influence on the recent U.S. election, digital voting has long been suspected of being both unreliable and highly vulnerable to tampering. Blockchain technology offers a way of verifying that a voter's vote was successfully sent while retaining their anonymity. It promises not only to reduce fraud in elections but also to increase general voter turnout as people will be able to vote on their mobile phones. Blockchain technology is still very much in its infancy and most of the applications are a long way from general use. Even Bitcoin, the most established blockchain platform, is subject to huge volatility indicative of its relative newcomer status. However, the potential for blockchain to solve some of the major problems we face today makes it an extraordinarily exciting and seductive technology to follow. I will certainly be keeping an eye out.

Why Bitcoin?

Bitcoin is known as the very first decentralized digital currency, they're basically coins that can send through the Internet. 2009 was the year when bitcoin was born. The creator's name is unknown, however the alias Satoshi Nakamoto was given to this person.

Bitcoin transactions are made directly from person to person through the internet. There is no need of a bank or clearinghouse to act as the middle man. Thanks to that, the transaction fees are way too much lower, they can be used in all the countries around the world. Bitcoin accounts cannot be frozen, prerequisites to open them don't exist, same for limits. Every day more merchants are starting to accept them. You can buy anything you want with them.

It's possible to exchange dollars, euros or other currencies to bitcoin. You can buy and sell, as it were any other country currency. In order to keep your bitcoins, you have to store them in something called wallets. These wallet are located in your pc, mobile device, on paper or in third party websites. Sending bitcoins is very simple. It's as simple as sending an email. You can purchase practically anything with bitcoins.

Bitcoin is a big deal right now, but not everyone understands why. More importantly, not everyone understands whether or not Bitcoin is for them, and how they can get involved. Here are some of the most compelling reasons why you should use Bitcoin.

More secure than banks

The Bitcoin algorithm is as close to bulletproof as a computer program can get. Some of the best hackers and online security experts have taken a crack at it, and so far no one can find any weaknesses. The Bitcoin code has been described as masterfully written, the digital equivalent to Shakespeare.

Bank transactions, meanwhile, are under a lower level of security than Bitcoin. In many ways, Bitcoin is more secure than keeping money in the banks. That makes Bitcoin a target for those who would like to see it fail. But Bitcoin's inventor Satoshi Nakamoto kept this in mind while writing the Bitcoin algorithm. Go ahead, give it a shot. I don't think you will be able to crack it.

Lower service fees than banks

Banking institutions charge high rates per transaction. The system is set up in a way that individual transactions between two people are impossible; they require a "trusted" third party to facilitate the transaction. And, naturally, the banks get to take a service fee for facilitating these transactions.

You can use escrow services with Bitcoin which take a service fee, but you don't have to. Because Bitcoin is based on P2P transactions, there are no service fees. Naturally, the banks aren't a big fan of Bitcoin because of this.

Low risk of inflation

Bitcoin volatility refers to how much the Bitcoin price jumps up and down over time.

This is a mathematical measure of the potential size of likely price changes. Relative volatility expectations explain why a 2% daily change in the value of a major currency may shock markets

Cryptocurrencies

whereas a 4% daily move in Bitcoin is considered standard.

Although the current Bitcoin volatility on the trading markets is very high, in the long run the risk of inflation is small. The number of Bitcoins being created is set at a predetermined rate. What that means is there is no possibility of any government printing off more money to pay off their debts. When the usage of this cryptocurrency becomes more common, the demand will rise and so will the price.

Whereas real world currencies lose a small percent of their worth every year. When your currency is attached to a government, it depends on the stability of that government. You and I both know governments can fall, and when they do the currency they printed can sometimes become worthless. Take a look at the bills in your wallet. You worked hard for them. Can you imagine them one day becoming worth less than the paper they were printed on?

Bitcoin isn't perfect. Just like anything, there are risks involved. In the face of increasing uncertainty in the global market, Bitcoin seems to be quickly becoming a beacon of stability and an exciting opportunity to create a new financial world.

Other characteristics of Bitcoin

Bitcoin has the characteristics of traditional currencies such as purchasing power, and investment applications using online trading instruments. It works just like conventional money, only in the sense that it can only exist in the digital world.

One of its unique attributes that cannot be matched by Fiat currency (Fiat currency is legal tender whose value is backed by the government that issued it. The U.S. dollar is fiat money, as are the euro and many other major world currencies) is that it is decentralized. The currency does not run under a governing body or an institution, which means it cannot be controlled by these entities, giving users full ownership of their bitcoins.

Bitcoin Anonymity

When doing a Bitcoin transaction, there's no need to provide the real name of the person. Each one of the bitcoin transactions are recorded is what is known as a public log. This log contains only wallet IDs and not people's names, so basically each transaction is private. People can buy and sell things without being tracked.

Moreover, transactions occur with the use of Bitcoin addresses, which are not linked to any names, addresses, or any personal information asked for by traditional payment systems.

Every single Bitcoin transaction is stored in a ledger anyone can access, this is called the blockchain. If a user has a publicly used address, its information is shared for everyone to see, without its user's information of course.

Bitcoin innovation

Accounts are easy to create, unlike conventional banks that requests for countless information, which may put its users in jeopardy due to the frauds and schemes surrounding the system.

Furthermore, Bitcoin transactions fees will always be small in number. Apart from near-instant completion of processing, no fees are known to be significant enough to put a dent on one's account.

Bitcoin established a whole new way of innovation. The Bitcoin software is all open source, this means anyone can review it. A nowadays fact is that bitcoin is transforming world's finances similar to how web changed everything about publishing. The concept is brilliant. When everyone has access to the whole Bitcoin global market, new ideas appear. Transaction fees reductions is a fact of bitcoin. Accepting Bitcoins cost anything, also they're very easy to setup. Charge backs don't exist. The Bitcoin community will generate additional businesses of all kinds.

JOHAN VON AMSTERDAM

What is a Bitcoin wallet?

A Bitcoin wallet is a piece of software that contains the "keys" and the address that allows you to send and receive bitcoins.

In the same way that Paypal uses an email address, the bitcoin protocol uses an address like 1JArS6jzE3AJ9sZ3aFij1BmTcpFGgN86hA extracted from the public keys stored in your wallet.

Most bitcoins are stored in what is called digital wallets. These wallets exist in the cloud or in people's computers. A wallet is something similar to a virtual bank account. These wallets allow persons to send or receive Bitcoins, pay for things or just save the Bitcoins. Opposed to bank accounts, these bitcoin wallets are never insured by the Federal Deposit Insurance Corporation (FDIC). The FDIC insures the deposits of bank customers against bank failure. The insurance premium is paid by nationally licensed banks to FDIC and they pay out benefits in the event of a bank going down.

The FDIC's mission is to protect depositors in the event of a bank failure, and maintain citizens' confidence in the banking system. When a bank fails, FDIC steps in and first attempts to get another bank to take over, for example when JP Morgan took over Washington Mutual.

In this book we'll show you the main types of wallets and how to create one step by step with blockchain.info.

Have you ever wondered how to step in into the bitcoin world?

You are in the right place.

Types of Bitcoin Wallet

A Bitcoin wallet is like to your bank account. It is used a to store, send and receive Bitcoins. A Bitcoin wallet stores the private keys and public keys. The public key is used to send/receive money and the private key is what actually gives you access to your account. Below are different types of Bitcoin wallet you can use.

Web or Wallet in the cloud

The most used and the easiest to set up.

It's accesible through your web browser and it's stored in the servers of the service provider.

It works in the same way as typical email clients, like Gmail or Yahoo.

Wallet in cloud: the advantage of having a wallet in the cloud is that people don't need to install any software in their computers and wait for long synchronizing processes. The disadvantage is that the cloud may be hacked and people may lose their bitcoins. Nevertheless, these sites are very secure. Be very careful with like drag and drop of documents into the cloud storage folder this could permanently move the document instead do copy and paste and accessibility; if you have no internet connection, you have no access to your data.

Desktop

They are installed on your computer and allow you to fully control the wallet because private keys are stored locally.

There are two types:

Full Clients, which download the entire blockchain and Lightweight Clients, that store the private keys locally but they don't download the entire blockchain, accessing to it through proxy servers.

The advantage of having a wallet on the computer is that people keep their Bitcoins secured from the rest of the internet. The disadvantage is that people may delete them by formatting the computer or because of viruses.

Mobile

They can work as Full Clients, Lightweight Clients or Web Clients.

Some of them are cross-platform, linked with web or desktop clients, sharing the same source of bitcoins.

Hardware

As pendrives, paper wallets or some other device types.

How to Create a Bitcoin Wallet

The easiest and fastest way to get started in the bitcoin world is by creating a web wallet.

There are several well proven providers as Coinbase or Blockchain. Both provide web wallets, an android app and an iPhone app.

In this guide we will use the blockchain web wallet due to its ease of use, simplicity and popularity.

Creating the Wallet

Go to blockchain.info and press "Create Wallet".

You will be asked for an email address that will be used to verify your identity each time you try to open your wallet (optional) and a password.

It is important to use a password as strong as you can think of with more than 10 characters, low and uppercase letters, numbers and symbols.

When finished, you will be asked to write and store a phrase that will be used to get access to your wallet if you forget your password.

This is important because there is no way to recover it if you lose your password.

Accessing the wallet

Once created and verified through the confirmation email, you are set to open it and start operating with Bitcoins.

To do it you have to introduce the identifier included in the mail and the password.

Once inside you will see the control panel of your wallet from which you can access your transaction history, the options for sending and receiving Bitcoins, the account settings and several options for backing up your wallet, something extremely important.

Receiving money

The first thing to do to receive bitcoins in your wallet is to know which your address is.

You can see it in the control panel of your wallet as a QR or as an alphanumeric code.

Share it so people can send you money through it.

Sending money

To send bitcoins you must click on the option and indicate the direction to which you want to send them and the amount.

Buying Bitcoins from the market

To directly exchange your dollars or euros are other fiat currency you can choose the option buy Bitcoins. You will get the current rate and the transaction cost and if you proceed you can setup your SEPA bank account for European banks. This to avoid additional transactions costs. Both Visa and Mastercards are accepted. This is one of the most common used options if you want to invest in Bitcoins. At the moment the maximum amount per transaction is U$ 250,-.

Transaction History

You can view the transaction history and its details by clicking on "My Transactions".

Here you will see the pair of adresses, the date on which the operation was performed, the amount sent/received and the number of confirmations.

You already have the main tool that lets you step into the Bitcoin world.

About commissions, confirmations and thieves

Although compared to the traditional banking system operations bitcoins are much cheaper, faster and safer, that do not make them free, instant or impossible to intercept.

Commissions

When sending Bitcoins you will see that the amount received is slightly smaller than the amount sent.

These fees are the incentive for miners to provide computing power to the Bitcoin network and keep the system running.

You can adjust the commission when making shipping but keep in mind that if it's very low, the transaction will take longer to be confirmed.

Confirmations

To avoid fraud, transactions in the bitcoin protocol must be confirmed by the network.

The system is designed so that each block of transactions is mined in about 10 minutes.

Security

Both the Bitcoin protocol and the majority of wallets are equipped with security layers that prevent your money is accessible to "foreign friends" with ease.

However, no system is perfect.

Other ways to store your Bitcoins

You usually do not carry 3.000 $ in your pocket, right? Due to the same reasons you don't do this, the same applies to bitcoin.

You shouldn't store all your Bitcoins in the same place.

Luckily, there are several ways to do this and most of them free or at a low cost.

Two of the most common are:

Cold Storage: Cold storage refers to keep your Bitcoins offline. This can be done in different ways (link to knowledge base), as in servers disconnected from the network, USB flash drives or paper wallets.

Creating other wallets: You can create as many wallets as you want

Cryptocurrencies

and store in them the bitcoins you have. A common practice is to deposit a certain amount in the wallet more used to operate and leave the bulk of your bitcoins in another.

Getting Your First Free Bitcoins

Now that you have a wallet, you will, of course, want to test them out.

The very first place to go is http://faucet.Bitcoin.st/.

This is a website that gives out small amounts of bitcoin for the purpose of getting people used to using them. The original version of this was run by the lead developer of bitcoin, Gavin Andreson. That site has since closed and this site operates by sending out one or two advertisements a month. You agree to receive those messages by requesting the Bitcoins. Copy and paste your new bitcoin address and enter a phone number to which you can receive an SMS. They send out an SMS to be sure that people are not continuously coming back for more since it costs nothing to create a bitcoin address. They will also send out once or twice a month advertisement to support their operation. The amount they send it trivial: 0.0015 BTC (or 1.5 mBTC). However, they process almost immediately and you can check to see that your address and wallet are working. It is also quite a feeling to get that portion of a bitcoin. (Non-disclaimer: I have no connection with this site and receive nothing if you use them. I simply think they are a good way to get your feet wet).

Congratulations! You have just entered the bitcoin economy.

To get your feet a little wetter, you can go panning for gold. There are a number of services and websites out there that will pay you in bitcoin to do things like go to certain websites, fill out online surveys, or watch sponsored videos. These are harmless, and you can earn a few extra bitcoins this way, but it is important to remember that these are businesses that get paid when people click on the links on their sites. They are essentially kicking back a portion of what they get paid to you. There is nothing illegal, or even immoral about this (you might like what you see and make a purchase!), but they are frequently flashy and may not be completely straightforward. All the ones that I have tried (particularly bitvisitor.com) have paid out as advertised. It is interesting to experiment with these, but even with the likely rise in the value of Bitcoin, you won't become a millionaire doing this. So, unless you are an advertisement junkie, I would recommend you move on. If you would like to try, simply Google "free bitcoins" or something along those lines and you will find numerous sites.

Buying Bitcoin Hand-to-Hand

Finally, this is going to be the real test of Bitcoin. Can people easily trade them back and forth? If this can't happen, then there can't really be a bitcoin economy because retailers won't be able to use it. If retailers can't use it, what earthly good is it? Fortunately, this is not really a problem. iPhone is a bit of a hold out, but many smartphones have apps (mobile wallets) that will read QR codes and allow you to send bitcoin to whomever you want. You can also display a QR code of your address, or even carry a card in your wallet with your QR code to let people send Bitcoin to you. Depending on what kind of wallet you have, you can then check to see if the Bitcoins have been received.

A couple of things to note:

When you set up your wallet, if you click around a bit, you will see an option to pay a fee to speed transactions. This money becomes available to a bitcoin miner as he/she/they process Bitcoin information. The miners doing the work of creating blocks of information keeps the system up to date and secure. The fee is an incentive to the miner to be sure to include your information in the next information block and therefore "verify" it. In the short term, miners are making most of their money by mining new coins (check the section on What Are Bitcoins for more information about this). In the long term, as it gets harder to find new coins, and as the economy increases, the fees will be an incentive for miners to keep creating more blocks and keep the economy going. Your wallet should be set to pay 0 fees as a default, but if you want, you can add a fee to prioritize your transactions. You are under no obligation to pay a fee, and many organizations that process many small transactions (like the ones that pan for gold described above) produce enough fees to keep the miners happy.

In clicking around your wallet, on the transactions page or linked to specific transactions, you will see a note about confirmations. When you make a transaction, that information is sent out into the network and the network will send back a confirmation that there is no double entry for that Bitcoin. It is smart to wait until you get several confirmations before walking away from someone who has paid you. It is actually not very easy to scam someone hand-to-hand like this, and it is not very cost-effective for the criminal, but it can be done.

Where can you buy bitcoin like this?

Blockchain and Coinbase

Bitcoin is the pinnacle of mobile money. The Bitcoin apps are becoming increasingly popular. Programmers are moving into the market to meet the growing demand of making it easier to buy and sell Bitcoin.

Smartphones are our constant companions, and there are many Bitcoin wallet apps on the Google Play Store, but the issue is finding one that fits your particular needs.

The Wallet you set up in chapter 6 on *Blockchain* is also accessible through downloadable Google Play Store and the iPhone App Store apps.

The other platform mentioned before, *Coinbase*, was founded in 2012. It also has apps for both iOS and Android, and it has inbuilt wallets for bitcoins, ether, litecoins and the good old US dollar. The wallet require a three-step verification process in order to access the Coinbase app. The Coinbase app also shows nice graphs about the market value of the cryptocurrencies, the last hour, the last 24 hours, the last week, the last month and the last year.

It requires an extensive identity verification process during signup, documents such as Proof of ID and residency have to be sent over and reviewed, similar to opening a bank account.

The app is incredibly user friendly, and can instantly convert Bitcoins, ethereum and litecoins to dollars and other fiat currencies and vice versa by using its built-in wallets for both currencies.

We have other mobile apps like:

- Copay
- Mycelium
- Bitpay
- Gliph
- Spare
- Fold and so on.

You may have a bitcoin Meetup in your area.

You can check out localbitcoins.com to find people near you who are interested in buying or selling.

Some are trying to start up local street exchanges across the world. These are called Buttonwoods after the first street exchange

Cryptocurrencies

established on Wall Street in 1792 under a buttonwood tree. See if there is one, or start one, in your area.

See if you have any friends who would like to try bitcoins out. Actually, the more people who start using bitcoin, the larger and more successful it will be come. So please tell two friends!

Some people ask if it is possible to buy physical bitcoins. The answer to this is both a yes and a no. Bitcoin, by its very nature, is a digital currency and has no physical form. However, there are a couple of ways that you can practically hold a bitcoin in your hands:

Cascascius Coins: These are the brainchild of Mike Caldwell. He mints physical coins and then embeds the private keys for the bitcoins inside them. You can get the private key by peeling a hologram from the coin which will then clearly show that the coin has been tampered with. Mike has gone out of his way to ensure that he can be trusted. These are a good investment strategy as in the years to come it may be that these coins are huge collector's items.

Paper Wallets: A paper wallet just means that rather than keeping the information for your bitcoin stored in a digital wallet, you print the key information off along with a private key and keep it safe in a safe, in a drawer, or in your mattress (if you like). This is highly recommended and cost effective system for keeping your Bitcoin safe. Keep in mind, though, that someone could steal them or if your house burns, they will go with the house and there will be no way to get them back. Really, no different than cash. Also, as with Casascius Coins, they will not really be good for spending until you put them back into the computer.

- There is software to make printing your paper wallets easier. bitcoinpaperwallet.com is one of the best and includes a good tutorial about how to use them.

- The bitcoins are not actually in the wallet, they are still on the web. In fact, the outside of the wallet will have a QR code that will allow you ship coins to the wallet any time you like.

- The sealed part of the wallet will have the private key without which you cannot access the coins. Therefore, only put as many coins on the wallet as you want to be inaccessible. You will not be able to whip this thing out and take out a few coins to buy a cup of coffee. Rather, think of it as a piggy bank. To get the money, you have to smash it. It is possible to take out smaller amounts, but at this point the security of the wallet is compromised and it would be easier for someone to steal the coins. Better to have them all in or out.

- People who use paper wallets are usually security conscious, and there are a number of ways for the nefarious in the world to hack your computer. Bitcoinpaperwallet.com gives a lot of good advice about how to print your wallets securely.

Some people have also asked about buying Bitcoins on eBay. Yes, it is possible, but they will be far overpriced. So, selling on eBay might seem to be a better option given the extreme markup over market value you might see. But, as with anything that is too good to be true, this is too good to be true. Selling bitcoin this way is just way too risky.

Bitcoin Investment Strategy

Apart from its abilities to purchase goods and services, one of its known applications features its use for a number of investment vehicles. This includes Forex (is a decentralized global market where all the world's currencies trade) trading Bitcoins, and binary options platforms. Furthermore, brands offer services that revolve around Bitcoin as currency.

Clearly, Bitcoin is as flexible as traditional legal tenders. Its introduction provides every individual with new beneficial opportunities with its ease of use and profit making capabilities. While the initial introduction of the technology came with a desktop program, it can now be directly operated through a smartphone application, which allows you to immediately buy, sell, trade or even cash your bitcoins for dollars.

This digital rush of money that is sweeping the global investors is not only getting easier, but also riskier everyday. While it was initially a simple peer-to-peer system for small transactions, it is now used for major investments and foreign luxury purchases, which has introduced newer strategies and uses. How does it really work?

The value

It is common knowledge it is improving the way transactions are being settled. The Bitcoin value relies heavily on how well the transaction fees are minimized; way below the transaction costs prevailing in the market. A professional broker understands better the value, which can help a great deal in ensuring sustained profits.

The positive feedback being submitted daily on the benefits of brokers is creating a lot of enthusiasm. Many companies are relying on brokers because of the vast potential present within the arena of crypto currency. The system offers a quick and efficient way of executing financial transactions

Investment with Bitcoins has become very popular, with major sums of money being put in every day. As a new investor, the rules remain the same as investing with real cash. Do not invest more than you can afford to lose, and do not invest without a goal. For every trade, keep certain milestones in mind. The 'buy low and sell high' strategy is not as easy implemented as said. A great way to succeed faster when you decide to trade bitcoins, however, is to learn the technicalities. Like cash investments, there are now several bitcoin charting tools to record the marketing trends and make predictions to help you make investment decisions. Even as a beginner, learning how to use charting tools and how to read charts can go a long way. A normal chart will usually include the opening price, the closing price, the highest price, the lowest price and the trading range, which are the essentials you need before making any sale or purchase. Other components will give you different information about the market. For example, the 'order book' contains lists of prices and quantities that bitcoin traders are willing to buy and sell.

Moreover, new investors will often quickly open unprofitable positions. With this, however, remember that you have to pay an interest rate for every 24 hours that the position is kept open, with the exception of the first 24 hours that are free. Therefore, unless you have sufficient balance to cover the high interest rate, do not keep any unprofitable position open for more than 24 hours.

Cryptocurrencies

While Bitcoin trading still has its drawbacks, like transactions taking too long to complete and no reversing option, it can benefit you greatly with investing, provided that you take small steps in the right direction.

Bitcoin Volatility

Traders are always concerned about 'Bitcoin''s volatility. It is important to know what makes the value of this particular digital currency highly unstable. Just like many other things, the value of 'Bitcoin' also depends upon the rules of demand and supply. If the demand for 'Bitcoin' increases, then the price will also increase. On the contrary side, the decrease in demand for the 'Bitcoin' will lead to decreased demand. In simple words, we can say that the price is determined by what amount the trading market is agreed to pay. If a large number of people wish to purchase 'Bitcoin's, then the price will rise. If more folks want to sell 'Bitcoin's, then the price will come down.

It is worth knowing that the value of 'Bitcoin' can be volatile if compared to more established commodities and currencies. This fact can be credited to its comparatively small market size, which means that a lesser amount of money can shift the price of 'Bitcoin' more prominently. This inconsistency will reduce naturally over the passage of time as the currency develops and the market size grows.

After being teased in late 2016, 'Bitcoin' touched a new record high level in the first week of the current year. There could be several factors causing the 'Bitcoin' to be volatile. Some of these are discussed here.

The Bad Press Factor

'Bitcoin' users are mostly scared by different news events including the statements by government officials and geopolitical events that 'Bitcoin' can be possibly regulated. It means the rate of 'Bitcoin' adoption is troubled by negative or bad press reports. Different bad news stories created fear in investors and prohibited them from investing in this digital currency. An example of bad headline news is the eminent utilization of 'Bitcoin' in processing drug transactions through Silk Road which came to an end with the FBI stoppage of the market in October 2013. This sort of stories produced panic among people and caused the 'Bitcoin' value to decrease greatly. On the other side, veterans in the trading industry saw such negative incidents as an evidence that the 'Bitcoin' industry is maturing. So the 'Bitcoin' started to gain its increased value soon after the effect of bad press vanished.

Fluctuations of the Perceived Value

Another great reason for 'Bitcoin' value to become volatile is the fluctuation of the 'Bitcoin''s perceived value. You may know that this digital currency has properties akin to gold. This is ruled by a design decision by the makers of the core technology to restrict its production to a static amount, 21 million BTC. Due to this factor, investors may allocate less or more assets in into 'Bitcoin'.

News about Security Breaches

Various news agencies and digital media play an important role in building a negative or positive public concept. If you see something being advertised Advantageously, you are likely to go for that without paying much attention to negative sides. There has been news about 'Bitcoin' security breaches and it really made the investors think twice before investing their hard earned money in 'Bitcoin' trading. They become too susceptible about choosing any specific 'Bitcoin' investment platform. 'Bitcoin' may become volatile when 'Bitcoin' community uncovers security susceptibilities in an effort to create a great open source response in form of security fixes. Such security concerns give birth to several open-source software such as Linux. Therefore, it is advisable that 'Bitcoin' developers should expose security vulnerabilities to the general public in order to make strong solutions.

The latest 'OpenSSL' weaknesses attacked by 'Heartbleed' bug and reported by Neel Mehta (a member of Google's security team) on April 1, 2014, appear to had some descending effect on the value of 'Bitcoin'. According to some reports, the 'Bitcoin' value decreased up to 10% in the ensuing month as compared to the U.S. Dollar.

Small option value for holders of large 'Bitcoin' Proportions

The volatility of 'Bitcoin' also depends upon 'Bitcoin' holders having large proportions of this digital currency. It is not clear for 'Bitcoin' investors (with current holdings over $10M) that how they would settle a position that expands into a fiat position without moving the market severely. So 'Bitcoin' has not touched the bulk market adoption rates that would be important to give option value to large 'Bitcoin' holders.

Effects of Mt Gox

The recent high-profile damages at 'Mt Gox' are another great reason for the 'Bitcoin' volatility. All these losses and the resultant news about heavy losses had a dual effect on instability. You may not know that this reduced the general float of 'Bitcoin' by almost 5%. This also created a potential lift on the residual 'Bitcoin' value due to the reason of increased scarcity. Nevertheless, superseding

Cryptocurrencies

this lift was the negative outcome of the news series that followed. Particularly, many other 'Bitcoin' gateways saw the large failure at Mt Gox as an optimistic thing for the long-term prospects of the 'Bitcoin'.

Tips for new Bitcoin traders

Investors from around the globe are trying to cash in on the volatile Forex market, by trading with the crypto-currency, Bitcoin. Well, it is quite easy to get started with onlinetrading, but it is important for you to know that there are risks involved that you cannot afford to overlook.

As with any of the speculative or exchange markets, Bitcoin trading is also a dicey venture, which can possibly cost you a lot of money, especially if you don't get it right. Therefore, it is essential for you to know about the risks involved, before deciding to get started with it.

If you are a newbie, who is interested in trading with Bitcoin, then you will need to first understand the basics of trade and investing.

Avoid the common errors that new traders generally tend to make

Invest wisely

Any kind of financial investment can bring losses, instead of profits. Similarly, with the highly unstable Bitcoin market, you can expect both, profits and losses. It is all about making the right decisions at the right time.

Most of the beginners tend to lose money by making the wrong decisions that are generally driven by greed and poor analytical skills. Experts say that you should not venture into trading, if you are not ready to lose money. Basically, such an approach helps you in coping up mentally for the worst possibilities.

Diversify the portfolio

First, successful traders diversify their portfolios. Risk exposure increases if most of your funds are allocated for a single asset. It becomes harder for you to cover the losses from other assets. You cannot afford to lose more money than you invested, so avoid placing more funds on limited assets. It will help you sustain the negative trades to quite an extent.

Secondly, putting in more cash than you can afford, will also cloud your sound decision making abilities. In most cases, you will be compelled to opt for 'desperate selling' when market declines a little. Rather than holding through the market dip, the investor who has over-invested on the trade, is bound to panic. The person will feel the urge sell off the holding for a low price, in an attempt to lessen the losses.

You will also be losing more cash, when market recovers. It is because you will have to buy the same holding back, but at higher price.

Set goals - Emotions make you blind

Goal setting for each transaction is vital when you trade Bitcoin. It helps you stay level-headed even in the extremely volatile conditions. Therefore, you will need to first determine the price to stop your losses.

The same rule also applies for profits, especially if you let your greed take over. The benefit of setting goals is that you can easily prevent making the decisions based on emotions.

Instead, you should work towards improving your skills for reading the charts and conducting the market analysis. It is also advisable for new traders to close their losing positions in 24 hours, so as to avoid paying the recurring interest.

If Bitcoin gets a adopted by big companies and a wider audience will try the acquire them, then prices will rise even more. Personally, I am in for the long run and will wait a couple of years. I have set a date and / or price for which I will sell a part of my cryptocurrencies. What ever comes first. In the meanwhile I try to keep my emotions under control.

Why should you start buying small amounts for the future?

As mentioned there will be only a fixed amount of Bitcoins available. Bitcoin is around for many years already and more and more companies and countries accept it as a method for payments. The demand keeps rising and the exchange rates also. If you buy them now and keep them, before Bitcoin goes mainstrain, you can still make big profits is my personal view.

But of course this is a personal decision and nobody knows for sure what will happen with the future supply and demand of these currencies, hence what will happen with the price. So I strongly suggest that if you want to invest to only invest money you can actually miss if things not turn out as expected.

Conclusion

Bitcoin is a decentralized peer to peer crypto-currency, and the first of its kind. It is one of the most fascinating innovations in finance in at least the last hundred years. Bitcoin is completely determined by an algorithm and everything is open-source so there are no surprises. No central agency can control the supply of Bitcoin, unlike fiat currencies or even materials like gold. The world can only ever see a total of 21 million Bitcoins in existence.

Like any new disruptive innovation, Bitcoin has a fiercely loyal core group of supporters and followers who are passionate about the idea. They are the ones who take it forward and spread the idea and take it to the next level. Bitcoin has plenty of enthusiasts who are excited about the idea and how it can shape the future of finance, giving the power of money back to the masses instead of under a central control.

It is not just a passing fad. Bitcoin is here to stay. Miners are gearing up for the best of the best equipment to mine Bitcoin more effectively. Exchanges are investing heavily in the security and efficiency of the Bitcoin system. Entrepreneurs are taking their chances and building great businesses around this idea. Venture capital funds are beginning to support projects that revolve around Bitcoin.

There are plenty of scenarios, black swan and otherwise where Bitcoins can become a dominant force in the financial industry. There are plenty of doom and gloom scenarios you can think of where Bitcoin will retain it's worth and value as hyperinflation consumes the fiat currency of a weak central government (there has been at least one recorded case in Argentina where a person sold his house for Bitcoin). However, that's being too pessimistic. Even without anything bad happening, Bitcoin can happily live alongside the traditional currencies of the world.

Some of the greatest advantages of Bitcoin are realized in efficient markets. It can be broken down into a hundred million parts, each called a satoshi, as opposed to fiat that usually can be broken down only into a hundred parts. Also, transactions over this network are essentially free or sometimes need a small transaction fee to induce the miners. By small, we are talking about less than a tenth of a percent. Compare this to the 2-4% fee charged normally by the credit card companies and you being to see why this concept is so attractive.

So now that you're convinced that Bitcoin is here to stay for the long run, how to make use of this? It is still in very early stages of development and there are plenty of places where you can make some Bitcoin. Faucets, for example, are supported solely by advertising and captchas and don't have any catch - you enter your wallet id and you get free Bitcoins.

There are several other concepts from the Get-Paid-To world translated and made especially for the Bitcoin economy. For example, there are several ways in which you can take surveys, watch videos, and visit advertiser websites, all in exchange for some Bitcoins. This being new, it is a great way to test out the waters and secure some of these in the process. Remember that it is far easier to give away Bitcoins because micro-transactions are so convenient. There doesn't have to be a real minimum payout and even when there is, it is usually very minimal.

Cryptocurrencies

In order to participate in the Bitcoin economy, you don't need to be a technical expert or even delve very deep into the workings of the currency. There are several services you can use to make the process as simple as possible. In this book we mentioned the Blockchain and Coinbase Apps and websites, were you can exchange your Euros or US Dollars for Cryptocurrenices like Bitcoin. It is all up to you to take that leap of faith and stay in the game for the long run.

Part 2: Bitcoin Cash versus Bitcoin

The battle of the cryptocurrencies

- Do you know the difference between Bitcoin and Bitcoin Cash?
- Which one is the most future proof?
- If you have bitcoin do you have Bitcoin Cash?
- Which exchanges support it?

2017 witnessed an important date in the history of cryptocurrency: the split that has created Bitcoin (BTC) and Bitcoin Cash (BCH).

Once a unified currency, Bitcoin now has new competition from a twin brother, Bitcoin Cash, which is leaving even the savviest of investors questioning what the difference really is and which is better.

An essential guide for any cryptocurrency investor, this book will address the major questions about this split and then look to the future for answers about what's next. A simple walk through a complicated minefield, you will discover Bitcoin's exciting history, the hidden features, and the most important underlying principles of this type of investing.

Cryptocurrencies

Get Answers to Questions Like:

- Where did Bitcoin come from?
- What exactly is Bitcoin Cash?
- What is the best investment?
- What does the future hold?
- How do I get started?
- Where to buy it?
- How to store?

Solve the mystery between cryptocurrency's major split and learn how to make smart investments with BTC and BCH.

Introduction

In recent times, the world of cryptocurrency has been gripped by the ever-growing rift with regard to how Bitcoin (BTC), the most successful cryptocurrency in history, can be improved. The Kafkaesque nature of the controversy resulted in a hard fork on the 1st of August 2017, which, in turn, brought about a split in Bitcoin (BTC) to what is now known as Bitcoin Cash (referred to as BCH or BCC[1]) and BTC (the original Bitcoin) itself. But what is the difference between these two currencies and what does this mean for new investors who are willing to stake their money on both Bitcoins, and what are the short and long term implications of these events for the average holders of these currencies?

- The most common abbreviation for Bitcoin cash is BCH, but sometimes also BCC is used to refer to Bitcoin cash.

- In this book only BCH will be used further on when referencing to Bitcoin cash.

Profoundly, this book not only seeks to address a lot of these issues but serves as an essential guide for beginners in cryptocurrencies, especially Bitcoin. Amazingly, it simply walks the reader through the history and features of cryptocurrencies, the underlying principles behind their operation, what makes Bitcoin tick, among several other important issues. With Bitcoin increasingly gaining traction in usage all over the world, it is pertinent to note that people are less likely to invest their money in any venture they know virtually nothing about; as a result, this book is designed to make critical information as simple as possible for new and existing investors.Furthermore, it is meant to serve as a quick guide to Bitcoin Cash, were to buy and store it.

Introduction to Cryptocurrencies

What Is Cryptocurrency

A cryptocurrency can be defined as a part of alternative currencies, virtual cash or digital asset that is intended for use as a medium of exchange while employing the use of cryptography as a technique to secure transactions and to take the creation of other units of the currency under management and control. For the sake of clarity, cryptography is the study of methods of creating and evaluating protocols that put a stop to third parties from reading concealed messages.

The History Of Cryptocurrencies

The forerunners of today's cryptocurrencies are the "b-money," which was a proposal and concept in the late 90s on a digital monetary system published by Wei Dai, a computer Engineer, and the "Bit Gold," a precursor of Bitcoin that was created by Nick Szabo. In fact, Wei Dai's work and ideas were identical to the Bitcoin scheme in use today, but he insisted that the concepts were developed independently of one another.

In 2009, a mysterious developer that goes by the pseudonym Satoshi Nakamoto created the first decentralized cryptocurrency, which is the bitcoin. Consequently, other cryptocurrencies such as Litecoin, Peercoinwas, Namecoin, Zcash, Dash, Ethereum, Rippx among several others have since come on board. Each of them has a broad range of features that seek to address specific issues plaguing the world of cryptocurrency.

Features

- Owing to the technology and security attributes they possess, it is hard to make counterfeits of cryptocurrencies.

- Another essential characteristic of cryptocurrencies that might make them more appealing is the fact that they are organic; in essence, it means that they are not created by a government or Central authority.

- What being decentralized means in effect is that they are, in theory, free from any form of meddling or manipulation.

- Unlike centralized currencies, nearly all cryptocurrencies are supposed to reduce in production in due course. For instance, Bitcoin is never going to exceed a market cap of 21 million coins that will be in circulation over time.

- Although a variety of cryptocurrency specifications are obtainable today, nearly all of them are the result of any of two protocols referred to as proof –of-work or proof-of stake.

- Every cryptocurrency often relies on a community of miners that help validate and process transactions with the use of their ASIC machines. Without a doubt, the contributions of miners are immense and invaluable in the sustenance of the entire system.

- Due to the cryptographic technology behind it, the users of cryptocurrencies are afforded some degree of anonymity making it hard for law enforcement agencies to seize them, unlike centralized currencies.

The Pros And Cons Of Cryptocurrencies

- Cryptocurrencies ensure the secure transfer of funds is carried out with ease.

- When compared with the amount charged by traditional financial institutions for the transfer of funds, the transmission of funds via cryptocurrencies comes at negligible processing fees, which makes it even more appealing to users.

- The technology behind the Bitcoin's blockchain which is a sort of online ledger that helps maintain every transaction that's ever been carried out by means of Bitcoins is being explored by experts for its potentials in crowdfunding, online voting and efficient processing of payments that could bring about a reduction of transaction fees in the Banking industry.

- Due to the inherent nature of cryptocurrencies as virtual or digital money, which is lacking a centralized repository, their balances are more susceptible to complete obliteration during a system crash, especially if no backup is maintained. Furthermore, their online ledgers may be prone to attacks from hackers.

- The market prices of cryptocurrencies are dependent on sentiments that fuels supply and demand, thereby making the rate at which they are exchanged move backward and forward widely.

The Basics Of Bitcoin

As stated earlier, Bitcoin is a digital currency that was created in 2009 by Satoshi Nakamoto who mined the first Bitcoin circulation. Bitcoin is one of the pioneering cryptocurrencies that employ the use of a peer-to-peer payment technology to aid in facilitating immediate payments or transactions. Being a virtual currency like all cryptocurrencies, Bitcoin is not owned by banks, stock exchanges, organization, governments, and company.

The Workings Of Bitcoin

Bitcoin Essentials

- For new users to get familiarized with the use of Bitcoin, they must first obtain a Bitcoin wallet software that will help encrypt and maintain Bitcoin balances on either their computer or mobile phone devices.

- Since most wallet software is downloadable, all you have to do is to download and install it on your devices.

- As soon as you have installed wallet software on any device of your choice, you may generate a Bitcoin address and share them with people to make payment to you or for you to pay to them. Also, you can generate as many Bitcoin addresses as your need for them warrants, but a Bitcoin address must only be utilized on one occasion for your anonymity to be sustained.

- Afterward, the investor can purchase Bitcoins via other payment means like credit card or bank account and fill up their wallet with the Bitcoins

- The adoption of Bitcoin as a medium of exchange is fast gaining popularity as it can be employed to settle transactions at dentists, groceries, clothing stores, online retailers, vehicle purchases, restaurants, and even for property rentals.

- Aside from using it to make payments for purchases, you can also make a fortune from speculating in Bitcoin itself. Such speculation centers on staking Bitcoins in the hope that it will go up in value.

- The least unit of Bitcoin is the Satoshi and is gotten when Bitcoin is dividable into eight decimal places, which is100 millionth of one Bitcoin. If the miners taking part agree to the change, Bitcoin could still be further split into more decimal places.

Understanding The Blockchain

A blockchain is the shared public ledger upon which the whole Bitcoin network is dependent and is a record of all transactions that's ever been carried out. The blockchain is regularly on the increase and being updated with fresh records of "blocks" that are deemed to have been 'completed.' To understand this above explanation clearly, you may consider it as a way of assessing the spendable balance of Bitcoin wallets and to verify new transactions to be Bitcoins that can be spent and are really owned by the individual spending them.

FEATURES OF THE BLOCKCHAIN

- The introduction of blocks to the blockchain is done in a linear, chronological order.

- Cryptography is used to ensure the security, integrity and chronological order of the blockchain system.

- Every computer (node) that is linked to the Bitcoin network with the intention of carrying out the validation and conveyance of transactions can automatically access a downloadable copy of the blockchain upon being linked with the Bitcoin network.

- It maintains full information concerning the addresses and their balances right from the origin of the block to the recently completed block.

How Does Blockchain Work?

The block itself is a 'current' aspect of a blockchain that accounts for some or all of the latest transactions, and as soon as it is complete, it moves straight to the blockchain as a long-lasting part of the database. The blockchain is an evidence of each one of such transaction on the Bitcoin network and can be viewed as a significant technological advancement of Bitcoin.

Every time a block becomes complete, a new one is created, and the blockchain has a limitless number of similar blocks in its system. You might want to think that the blocks are not well arranged or arbitrarily positioned in a blockchain, but, in reality, they are connected in an appropriate linear, chronological order, much in the same way chains are linked to one another, with each block holding a hash of the preceding block.

When drawing the comparison of the Bitcoin blockchain system with the traditional banking methods, blockchain can be likened to an entire record of a banking transaction. Another area of similarity is that transactions are chronologically inputted in a blockchain much in the same way bank transactions are entered. Furthermore, blocks can be likened to bank statements.

Every computer or node that takes part in the operation of the system can have access to the blockchain database and is dependent on the Bitcoin protocol in use. The complete copy of the blockchain contains detailed account and history of all Bitcoin transactions ever performed.

It can thus provide insight as regards detailed information on a specific Bitcoin address; such as how much worth or value can be attributed to it at any point in its history. The growing popularity of Bitcoin as a cryptocurrency has resulted in an enormous increase in transactions, and it is estimated that a new block is added to the block chain via mining at an average about 10 minutes apiece. It is important to note that the ever-rising size of the blockchain is regarded by some stakeholders as problems that arose out of storage and harmonization.

WHAT ARE BITCOIN BLOCKS?

Blocks can be defined as files in which data relating to the Bitcoin network is entered or recorded in a lasting manner. The block is designed in such a way that it takes account of several or every one of the most recent Bitcoin transactions that haven't been captured in any past blocks.

As a result, the block functions in the same way as a page of a bank ledger or record book. As soon as a block is deemed to be 'completed,' it gives up to the subsequent block in the blockchain. Another key feature of a block is that it maintains a lasting store of records, which as soon as it is written, can't be changed or gotten rid of.

In summary, since the Bitcoin network is subject to a significant amount of transactional activities, it becomes pertinent to keep an evidence of these transactions so that users can follow the trail of what's been paid, to whom and by whom. The block directly takes a record of transactions that's been carried out within a particular period.

Bitcoin Protocols

The inherent and underlying issues that are often associated with the traditional cryptocurrency made Bitcoin to come up with the use of the blockchain protocol to manage the entire system because Bitcoin is one of the first peer-to-peer payment networks that also works based on a cryptographic protocol. In reality, no particular individual can lay claim to ownership of the bitcoin protocol, but we shall examine the workings of the protocol and also take a look at the major Bitcoin protocols.

How Does Bitcoin Protocol Work?

Owners of Bitcoins can send and receive coins by just broadcasting digitally signed messages to the network via their bitcoin wallet's software. Since the existing Bitcoin transaction system is reliant on trust, users can only hope that each transaction will bring about a specific outcome. However, the issue is that these electronic payment systems are not to be relied on infrequently, thereby resulting in apprehension about fraud between buyers and sellers.

The problem of deceit or unreliability might be the result of a variety of factors that range from users trying to double-spend their coins or a user making an effort to refuse service from another user or a user looking for ways to exploit the system for financial gains. As a way of putting a check on the issues as mentioned earlier and other possible attacks that may arise; Bitcoin developers set up a system that is dependent on cryptographic proof via the utilization of digital signatures and a very complicated verification process.

Using Digital Signatures For Verification

Blockchain employs the use of a series of digital signatures known as "coin," that is received as soon as a holder passes it on to the next owner. Every time it is transferred, the owner inserts a hash that indicates the past transactions and the public key of the new holder. As the electronic coin goes from one owner to another, notations are all included at the end of it, so as to give a way to verify ownership.

Extra Layer Of Trust Using Timestamp Server And Proof-Of-Work System

As a way of ensuring that the same value of coins are not spent more than once or "double spent," Bitcoin developers set up a verification process that determines how the coin is being used. The process employs the use of a timestamp server that inserts a period in time to the hash to confirm or verify the transaction. In addition to that, the timestamp is integrated, together with each change in possession of the coin. Furthermore, a proof-of-work system applies a specific value to the electronic coin to further authenticate every transaction that is carried out with the cryptocurrency.

The Blockchain Network

As mentioned earlier, Bitcoin as a cryptocurrency is decentralized in the sense that it employs a network format whereby all new transactions are stored into blocks. Afterward, the value or a proof-of-work is added to the block and then relayed throughout the network. Acceptance of the blocks of digital coins is only possible after they have been confirmed valid and verified as being unspent.

New blocks will continue to go through the process of sustaining the movement of the digital coins from one owner to another and being tracked whether it has been spent on specific goods or services with the blockchain network which is also regarded as a kind of ledger. As soon as sufficient blocks are generated from the digital coins, they can then be gotten rid of, to make more disk space available to hold newer blocks.

LINKING CHAINS

Maintaining An Honest Ledger

Due to the common threat of fraud that the conventional transaction system was well-known for, it becomes essential for blockchain to try to find a way to make sure that those dealing with these blocks are as sincere as possible. What it means, in essence, is that, for those to whom the task of verifying and recording transactions (miners) on the block to remain honest and sincere, they are to be compensated by way of their digital coins as recompense for honest work.

This way, miners become conscious of the fact that, adhering to the regulations of blockchain a great deal is beneficial than to try and con the system. Miners are individuals or organizations with machines that verify a transaction and include it to the public blockchain so that other miners can have the right to use and bring up to date their own version of the blockchain. For their role and the work they carry out on the blockchain network, miners get rewarded with a little portion of each transaction they execute.

On the other hand, there are a number of backup procedures, which are often in operation on the network or business-owned machines that Bitcoin developers have adopted and enforced to thwart any attack or to prevent bad blocks from the network. A typical case in point of a backup course of action is network alerts which may have been fashioned to go off, once miners discover these bad blocks. Afterward, the alerts and doubtful blocks are pulled and evaluated for any contradictions and then taken out if they are discovered to be invalid.

How Blockchain Fosters Privacy And Anonymity

Bitcoin is able to guarantee the privacy of users because the blockchain technology only gives an idea that an individual is sending something to someone else without giving a clue about what is being sent and whether it has to do with currency, information, or any other form of valuable asset. The elimination of a dependable third party and counter party attaches a degree of privacy to the use of electronic cash for transactions. In this fashion, the process of employing the use of cryptocurrency such as Bitcoin gives the holder some degree of anonymity.

Major Bitcoin Protocols

The growth of Bitcoin as a cryptocurrency since its origin in 2009 has been on a meteoric rise both in size and scope with its notional value reaching in excess of $10 billion and so has its network grown at an exponential rate as well. All through this development, the system started to go through various pains linked to such growth, and they are widely related to scaling up, in order to create room for the huge number and rate of transactions, while maintaining the security, intrinsic worth of privacy, and reduced transaction costs all at once.

At this stage, it is crucial to bear in mind that the novel protocol that was written by Bitcoin's founder, the mysterious Satoshi Nakamoto has turned out to be known as Bitcoin core or Bitcoin QT. And it has led to three rival versions of the Bitcoin protocol; which are the BitPay Core, Bitcoin Classic and Bitcoin Unlimited. The three attempts came in the wake of a contentious roll out of Bitcoin XT that might have resulted in an increase of the block size to 8MB but were mostly rejected by the bitcoin community.

Bitpay Core

Although BitPay Core is in a trial phase for now, however, its fundamental concept revolves around having two limits. Number one is a 'hard limit' on block size that would be altered on a frequent basis, coinciding with intricate adjustments, and a second 'soft limit' which the miner community will want to make compulsory among themselves and is comparable to the focal points of Bitcoin Unlimited.

Bitcoin Classic

This Bitcoin protocol aims to take the edge off the issues of huge transactions that are leading to transaction log jams and rising transaction costs. The protocol hoped to achieve this by way of increasing the block size, which is the quantity of kilobyte in a block of transactions from 1MB to 2MB. The choice of 2MB was selected on purpose and was dependent on the results of data gathered by its developers, and from interactions with several Bitcoin miners and mining pools. Aside from the support, it has from big mining pools like AntPooland BW Pool, and wallet/exchanges such as Coinbase and OKCoin, the creators of Bitcoin classic states that they have the backing of Gavin Andresen, the past Bitcoin Core lead and Bitcoin XT developer.

Bitcoin Unlimited

This Bitcoin protocol as the name implies embraces the nonexistence of a hard-coded block-size limit. As a substitute, it lets users set limits on their nodes manually; the developers look ahead to a compromise on a limit to materialize naturally at an ostensibly Schelling or focal point. The protocol is designed to be a solution that people will be inclined to exploit in the absence of communication since it appears natural, unique, or valuable to them. In addition, it aims to bring in some degree of democracy by letting the community to vote on necessary changes regarding how to develop, manage and implement the protocol.

Bitcoin Private Keys

A Bitcoin private key can be described as a secret number created to let people spend their Bitcoins or make irreversible transactions. Users are given a Bitcoin private key when they are issued with a Bitcoin address. Typically, it has a 256-bit number and may be used to sell, accept, donate Bitcoin, hence must be kept really safe. For instance, a Bitcoin private key may look like this: *18Qs4IuA5d5ViEiPWYau6fhRTHEFZ9XaLo*.

Keeping Your Private Keys Safe

In the past, several secret/private keys or backup seed have been lost due to the storage medium on which they are saved. Frequently used mediums of storing private keys are listed below with some of their weaknesses

Storage On A Piece Of Paper

Whether the information is written, printed or laminated, a number of things could go wrong with the storage medium, and they are not limited to the following:

- The paper may be discovered and stolen
- The paper could be torn, burnt, spoiled, or damaged by smoke
- A hand-written paper might not be legible; laminated paper is susceptible to being ruined while attempts to print on paper could be unsuccessful if the paper is wet.

Storage On A Flash Drive

- The possibility of breakage exists

- It can be affected by fast changing magnetic fields, for example, MRIs

- They may be affected by fire and smoke

- Many of these drives are not designed for storing things in the long run

- Can become corroded from salt water or some atmospheric conditions

- You may find it hard to retrieve your data from it

- It can be adversely affected by harsh environmental factors

- In general, flash drives aren't recommended for long-term storage

Storage In The Cloud

- There is a risk of hackers attempting to steal the private keys

- Other people may have access to your cloud storage and take the keys

Storage On A Computer

- They are susceptible to crashes which make data recovery costly

- Computers are prone to physical attacks and may get burnt or damaged by smoke

- The data on conventional hard disc drive may be degraded by strong magnetic fields and could get destroyed physically.

- Mishaps might occur that will bring about data loss

- It is ill-advised to store up data meant to last for long on Solid state drives (SSDs) if they are not going to be powered.

- If the computer is linked to the internet, it is prone to attacks from hackers who might want to break into it, to steal the key irrespective of the encryption technology employed.

- The use of a computer for storage of private keys is often associated with a broad range of threats like firmware exploits, the use of malicious USB cords and 0-day exploits.

- The use external hard disk drives for storage are limited to just couple of years as a minimum if stored appropriately

- If computer is not linked to the net, the safety it provides is function of the encryption technology used and doesn't negate the fact that an individual may still enter the location illegally and copy the data with no one taking notice

STORAGE ON DIGITAL MEDIA LIKE CD, FLOPPY DISK, LASERDISC, OR MINI-DISC

- There is a high tendency for plastics to stop working after a while.

- Exposure to adverse environmental conditions such as heat, humidity, regular light, all kind of chemicals, and the oxygen in the air may degrade them. It could also result in data loss when private keys are stored on a medium derived from plastic or written/printed on plastic.

- Plastics could get burnt or become damaged by smoke

- The risk of bodily harm occurring exist, thereby making it not viable or costly to recover the lost data

- There is a probability that magnetic media such as tapes and floppy disc could be damaged by magnetic fields

Cryptocurrencies

Between A Hard And A Soft Fork!

Since Bitcoin operates, based on open source software, which implies that the code is free and accessible for everyone to view and make use of. On the other hand, for individuals or organizations hoping to take part in the Bitcoin network whether as miners, node operators, or wallet administrators; the update and maintenance of the existing versions of the Bitcoin software code vary from essential to very necessary.

With the evolution of Bitcoin as a cryptocurrency, it becomes imperative that several adjustments have to be made to the protocol. These alterations may range from including new feature sets like allowing multi-sig, to altering a core metric of the protocol, such as raising the peak block size.

The Elephant In The Room

The core issue is with the speed of the technology which is really slow. Bitcoin network processes around seven transactions in 10 minutes compared to VISA that handles 150 million transactions every day. VISA deals with 1700 transactions per second, and its system has the ability to handle 24000 each second. Users of Bitcoin are increasing every day, and there's no alteration to the core technology that handles their transactions, thereby resulting in network logjams and extensive waiting period for transactions to go through.

The Rudiments Of Forks

It is important to note that before now, Bitcoin forks takes place somewhat on a regular basis. A fork is the side-effect of distributed consensus that occurs whenever two miners locate a block almost at the same time. To put it simply, a fork in software development alludes to an event that results in an independent project spinning off from a software project.

The resolution of the uncertainty around such events becomes apparent when successive blocks are added to one, thereby causing it to become the lengthiest chain, whereas the other block becomes "orphaned" or neglected by the network.

However, forks could as well be deliberately set up in the network, and often comes about when developers try to make amends to the rules that the software utilizes to make a decision on whether a transaction is valid or not. For instance, Litecoin, a cryptocurrency is a fork of Bitcoin since the creators of Litecoin copied Bitcoin's code, carried out some alterations, and then launched a separate project.

As soon as a block is found to have transactions that are invalid, then it is disregarded by the network, and the miner who discovers that block will miss out on a block recompense. Consequently, miners, in general, would like to mine only blocks that are valid and built on the longest chain. It is vital to keep in mind that changes induced to a protocol often call for either a soft or hard fork of the Bitcoin software. Performing a fork of the Bitcoin software is different from other open source projects since each user operating a Bitcoin node have to sustain their compatibility with the network.

The implication is that any miner that is making use of a Bitcoin software version that isn't suited to the version all and sundry are using may find themselves mining the wrong Blockchain. Nevertheless, miners may bring different versions of the Bitcoin software into play and mine the same Blockchain if the varying versions are well matched. Here, compatibility is very vital.

Below are some the more widely known forks and their characteristics:

Hard Fork

A hard fork can be described as a software upgrade that sets up a new rule to the network which isn't well-matched with the older software. It could be merely regarded as an extension of the rules. For example, a new rule that permits block size to be 2MB in place of 1MB would have need of a hard fork. A hard fork is complicated in nature as it is an alteration of the Bitcoin protocol, which isn't backward compatible with older versions of the client.

When a hard fork takes place, Nodes that keep on operating on the old version of the software will find newer transactions on the network as being invalid. However, for the entire community to carry on mining valid blocks, every single one of the nodes in the network would have to upgrade to the new rules.

What Are The Risks?

When a hard fork occurs, it could lead to a lot of issues that are not limited to the political fallout that may take place when some sort of political impasse arises, and a fraction of the community prefers to stand by the old rules come what may. In this case, the network computing power or hash rate behind the old chain makes no difference. In fact, what counts the most is the data rule set, since the data is still supposed to have value, which means miners are keen to mine a chain and developers are apt to prop it up. A typical case of how a community might be torn apart over rules is the

Ethereum DAO hard fork that resulted in two blockchains employing a variation of the software (Ethereum and Ethereum classic) with both having dissimilar philosophy and currencies.

When a hard fork is performed, the principal risk that may occur is a circumstance whereby nodes on the network using the new software are separated from the earlier version, leading to a fork of the Blockchain. For instance, you may find half of the nodes on the network are using the latest version and mining blocks while the remaining half are mining a different set of blocks by running the older version of the software; which in essence means you will get two dissimilar chains giving rise to a fork of the Blockchain. The scenario given above is quite different from a software fork.

Soft Fork

On the other hand, a soft fork is any alteration that is backward compatible. For example, a new rule could just let 500 Kilobyte blocks as an alternative to 1MB block. In this situation, nodes that have not been upgraded to be compatible with the new rule will see the new transactions as valid because 500 kilobyte is below 1MB in this scenario. But, should the nodes that haven't been upgraded to be compatible with the new rules keep on mining blocks, the blocks they mine won't be recognized by the nodes that have been updated and rejected as a result. It is for this reason that soft forks require a greater part hash power in the network.

What Are The Risks?

A soft fork that doesn't get a majority of hash power in the network implies that it has very little support and may turn out to be the shortest chain and thus, become orphaned by the network.

Otherwise, it may behave in the same vein as a hard fork whereby one chain might just break off. But, if members of the community find it hard to reach a consensus and are separated by such an issue, then the old and new version of Bitcoin might emerge as distinct projects from then on.

It is not all gloom with soft forks because they have mainly been the frequently used choice to upgrade the Bitcoin blockchain nearly all the time, as it is believed that they offer a lesser risk of tearing the network apart. In the past, some soft forks that have gone quite well consists of the P2SH that resulted in the alteration of Bitcoin's address formatting, and the BIP 66 that took care of Bitcoin's signature validation.

User-Activated Soft Fork (Uasf)

A user-activated soft fork (UASF) can be described as a contentious proposal that looks at the way a blockchain could add an upgrade, which isn't backed, directly by those stakeholders who makes the network's hashing or computing power available.

The concept of UASF aims to work on the basis that rather than wait for a threshold of support from mining pools, the authority to trigger a soft fork should go to the exchanges, wallets, and companies who are using full nodes. A full node is seen in Bitcoin as one that is still in charge of validating blocks, even though it may not be a mining node.

A greater fraction of key exchanges may have to publicly give their backing to the change, ahead of it being written into a new version of the code. Subsequently, the new software that has been assigned a starting point in the future becomes installed on nodes that would like to partake in the soft fork.

What Are The Risks?

This approach calls for a much longer lead time for it to work than a soft fork that is hash-power-triggered. In fact, it is assumed it could take as much as a year or more to write the code and get all and sundry geared up.

Additionally, if nearly all of the miners end up not agreeing to activate the new rules, they may bring into play their remarkable hash power to divide the network. At present this proposal is hypothetical and hasn't been put into operation.

BTC Versus BCH

Bitcoin (BTC) is the popular cryptocurrency that's known all over the world for many years, while in contrast, Bitcoin Cash (BCH) is the projected hard fork that maintained it is closest to Satoshi Nakamoto's original idea for the currency. In order words, BTC and BCH are probable forks of the Bitcoin blockchain.

Before August 1st, 2017 there was a huge debate over the validity of BCH because there was uncertainty whether mining organizations would begin to assign hashing power to it. A move that could end up making it a valid, usable currency with enhanced scalability than the real Bitcoin (BTC) itself, and might even surpass the price of Bitcoin swiftly and turn out to be the default online currency. Otherwise, it might end up being worthless or just like any alt coin out there.

The root of the problem pertains to Bitcoin's legacy code and its capacity of 1MB of data for each block, or around three transactions for every second. The debate had raged for over a year concerning a 'consensus' solution to the problem. Some few days earlier, most key members of, the community had agreed to an upgrade known as Segwit(Segregated Witness) that was locked-in to be wholly put into operation by November 2017.

However, BCH was at variance with the philosophy of Segwit and then made known its plan to increase the block size limit to 8MB by setting off the User Activated Hard Fork (UAHF) on August 1, 2017. Again, supporters of Bitcoin cash considered SegWit to be going against some essential strong points of Bitcoin, such as its decentralization and democratization.

Additionally, they also think SegWit2x was being led by persons with links to shady organizations, and that SegWit2x could be the end of Bitcoin as it is known.

BCH

With its proposal, Bitcoin Cash (BCH) plans to resolve these problems, and it is crucial to bear in mind that one of the most remarkable things about Bitcoin Cash (BCH) is that it gives room for custom block sizing. The increased block size of 8MB proposed by BCH is expected to speed up verification process, and ultimately ensure the survival of the network in spite of the number of miners backing it, albeit with some adjustable degree of difficulty. Its key features include:

- Bitcoin Cash is lead by a client that is referred to as BitcoinABC; where the ABC means "Adjustable Blocksize Cap." In essence, it implies that users may determine their favored blocksize as a result.

- The BCH's default blocksize is set to 2MB, and it has the potential for users to scale it up to 16MB.

- On its official website, BCH defines its currency as being the same as Satoshi's original vision for the coin. It goes on to affirm that *"Bitcoin Cash is peer-to-peer electronic cash for the Internet. It is entirely decentralized, with no central bank and requires no trusted third parties to operate."*

SEGWIT2X

As the August 1st deadline drew nearer, one of two key proposals for enhancing bitcoin's transactional capacity is the SEGWIT2X, which may have gained the most interest. It has the support of a considerable number of prestigious Bitcoin organizations and individuals, the majority of whom are directly associated with the system's startup and investment community. They include nearly all the network's big mining pools, prominent developers such as Gavin Andresen of Bitcoin Core, Bitcoin startups such as Blockchain, BitPay, and Coinbase, among several others.

Features

- SEGWIT was an optimization put forward by Bitcoin Core developer Pieter Wuille in 2015 that aims to increase the number of transactions that go into every block with no need to raise the block size parameter. In particular, it also takes away the problem of transaction malleability, which may result in a significant improvement of the network if resolved.

- The alterations proposed by SEGWIT2X seek to update the software rules to give room for 2MB blocks. Other rivals with similar objectives to raise Bitcoin's block size parameter such as Bitcoin Unlimited, Bitcoin XT and Bitcoin Classic do not have the same level support as SEGWIT2X.

- Before August 1st, 2017, SEGWIT2X wasn't suggested nor sanctioned by Bitcoin Core, the network's major open-source developer team.

- SEGWIT2X will perform long-anticipated code optimization Segregated Witness (SegWit) that changes the way some data is amassed on the network.

- Its ideas and proposals aren't as fresh but only bring together those proposed earlier by other developers in a new manner.

- As soon as SegWit is activated, it sets a timeline of three months (November 2017), to raise the network's block size from 1MB all the way up to 2MB.

Update

The primary aspect of SegWit2x known as BIP91was locked-in and triggered some days before the scheduled August 1, while BIP148 was to be set off on that day itself. Having locked-in BIP91, a lot of people believed the likelihood of a hard fork was over, but supporters of BCH seem to have other ideas.

The Split!

A TALE OF TWO Bitcoins

On the morning of August 1st, 2017, an attempt to generate another version of the bitcoin blockchain was formally making progress. After overcoming some obstacles that morning, miners managed to create a block on a new blockchain successfully, called Bitcoin Cash at 18:24:41 UTC.

- Then, ViaBTC pool created a 1.9 MB BCH block that wasn't valid on the legacy Bitcoin network. This move, in fact, marked a break away from the major bitcoin network and taking the lead with a different technical plan.
- In general, the event occurred almost six hours after block 478,558 – the point at which miners made efforts to begin the split.
- Data from the network reveals that the BCH block had 6,985 transactions, with a block size of 1.915 MB which was almost two times the size of this parameter on the original chain. The data point is noteworthy since BCH was intended to boost network capacity by providing a blockchain with a bigger block size.

Support From Bitcoin Providers

As long as your Bitcoins are securely held in a personal wallet, the likelihood of losing your cashcoins is very slim. But, there is a slim chance that malicious miners could attempt to pilfer your coins when you attempt to make Bitcoin transactions. In trying to prevent this risk from occurring you may have to divide the coins into different Bitcoin and Bitcoin Cash wallets. Some wallets have given specific updates, services, and instructions for splitting coins.

Ahead of the August 1st, 2017 events, some major exchanges, and wallet providers gave their strategy for the hard fork. Many stated that they wouldn't back BCH at all; some said they would support it as an altcoin that will let users split their coins if they want.

But none of the businesses affirmed that they would back BCH as the number one, genuine Bitcoin. As an alternative, they declared an intention to support Bitcoin itself, or endorse the longest chain, which means that they would support any of the blockchain that emerged triumphantly.

Below are a list of leading Bitcoin exchanges and their position on sustaining BCH trading dated August 2017.

- Coinbase: will reject BCH
- BitMEX: will reject BCH
- Bitstamp: will reject BCH
- Bittrex: agreed
- Kraken: agreed
- OkCoin: agreed
- Poloniex: Possibly
- BTCC: agreed

- Gemini: will wait to see if BCH is viable
- Fitbit: will reject BCH
- ViaBTC: Yes, at a 1:1 ratio

Important note:
The most of above Bitcoin exchanges, which initially rejected Bitcoin cash trading, are altered their vision after lawsuits and pressure from the Bitcoin user community and decided the support the trade of Bitcoin cash in the (near) future.

From its website, wallets that support Bitcoin cash (BCH) ahead of the 1st of August event include the following:

- BitcoinUnlimited
- BitcoinABC
- Ledger
- ElectrumCash
- FreeWallet
- BitcoinClassic
- BXT
- Trezor
- BTC.com
- AirBitz
- Coinomi

Some major wallets have the following opinion about BCH:

Blockchain.info

It is crucial that owners of Blockchain wallets retain their wallet and associated recovery phrase and not delete them, even though they may empty the BTC balance. It supports withdrawals from exchanges that won't support BCH.

Electrum

Despite the fact that the most recent version of Electrum, 2.9, is able to make a distinction between rival chains, Electrum doesn't back Bitcoin Cash formally. In reality, Electrum believes the "Electrum Cash" fork of their software to be a trademark violation.

Ledger

Ledger is a trendy hardware wallet that supports Bitcoin Cash. Also, its wallet interface will feature a split utility and a selector for the two chains.

Exodus

Exodus doubles as a wallet and exchange service outlet, and doesn't provide support for BCH, either via splitting or providing a market.

Jaxx

Users on this platform are usually in charge of their private keys, and matching Bitcoin Cash (BCH) ought to be secure in your Jaxx wallet. But, users have to bear in mind that they won't be able to access/send/receive their Bitcoin Cash (BCH) pending when the integration occurs.

Aftermath Of The Bitcoin Split

BTC And BCH

Some days after Bitcoin (BTC) had gone through an upgrade and a currency split, the foremost Cryptocurrency looks as if it has outlived one of the most tumultuous periods in its lifetime. The question you'd want to ask is, how has Bitcoin fared after this controversial and massive split? The outcome has thus far been splendid for Bitcoin. Everything appears to be getting back to normal, as confidence in the currency continues to soar with miners, traders, exchanges, and users of Bitcoin all going about their business as usual.

On the day that the split took place, the price of BTC which had been on a recovery to its former level a few days before August 1st, 2017, fell in value from $2,875 to $2718, representing about 5% drop. On the other hand, Bitcoin Cash (BCH) surpassed Ripple to turn out to be the third largest cryptocurrency, by trading at around $400 levels. Some few hours later BCH's price movement became livelier and was trading in the region of $700 and having a market capitalization that went past $11 billion, representing nearly11% of the general market capitalization.

The Impact Of The Split On`Etherium

Some days before the split, Bitcoin (BTC) dropped about 10% to below $2,500 level in value owing to uncertainty over the impending upgrade and split. But it on the 1st of August, Ethereum (ETH) experienced a rise that pushed it tidily clear of $220 levels.

What Does The Future Hold For BTC And BCH

As at the time of writing this ebook, Bitcoin (BTC) just flew past the $3,500 level, which indicates a high degree of confidence in the number one cryptocurrency. With the second phase of the implementation of its upgrade still looming ahead on 1st of November 2017, which is a hard fork that is not backward compatible with older Bitcoin clients and will double the Bitcoin's block size to 2MB. When the result is coupled with the increase in block size limit that SEGWIT will bring about, then Bitcoin (BTC) should have a total maximum of 8MB of block space.

If the upgrade goes according to plan, then Bitcoin should continue to soar. Expectedly, BTC ought to continue with its rise in value than other cryptocurrencies and keep on enjoying a majority of the market capitalization. Perhaps we might see it reaching the $5,000 before the end of the year. It should remain safe and secure to use, but it would be hard to tell how its processing speed will be like in future. Furthermore, if other stakeholders in the community feel some of the core principles of Bitcoin such as its decentralized nature and democratic potentials of the blockchain technology is being compromised, then they might move on to other cryptocurrencies that have exciting possibilities and appeals to them.

As for BCH, it is currently trading (august 2017) at $340 but may likely rise in value in due time, if it is able to get miners to invest sufficient hash power to its network. Several estimates have it that BCH is able to attract 4% of miners to itself, making it vulnerable to attacks from malicious actors who manage some of these computing powers, and the only way they can prevent such attacks

Cryptocurrencies

is to get close 50% of the Bitcoin's hash rate. That's why BCH's value might be just a fraction of BTC in the long run. However, if the SEGWIT changes make a lot of people unhappy, and they decide to switch over to BCH then its hash power might go up considerably.

Part 3: Monero versus Bitcoin

The battle of the cryptocurrencies

- Do want to diversify your bitcoin investments in other cryptocurrencies?

- Do you want to invest (more) in monero and / or bitcoin?

- Do you want to know where to start?

- Do you want of an overview of the exchanges where you can buy ripple?

- Do you want of an overview of the wallet-types and wallets to store your new investment?

- Do you want to make an educated decision and investment?

Start reading this part of the book

This part will help you make a well-informed decision about whether you should invest (more) in bitcoin, monero or whatever cryptocurrency for that matter.

Here you will learn:

- history of both cryptocurrencies

- the problems these cryptocurrencies were designed to solve

- if they meet those promises in reality (speed, ease of use, safety, security)

- a detailed description of the big exchanges were you can acquire bitcoin and ripple

Cryptocurrencies

- a profound explanation of the different type of wallets to store your new investments and safety guidelines

- AND an overview of the different investment strategies you can follow

In this section, you will find all the answers you have about these cryptocurrencies and learn new facts you did not even consider.

Introduction

Cryptocurrencies are a revolution, one that promises change not only to the financial markets but also to other industries and sectors. Their development has brought to the world a paradigm shift in the way things are done, a shift which is shaking up the status quo as well as the way issues are thought of and solved. The ingenuity behind the development of cryptocurrencies exudes both brilliance and the need to harness the power of technology to take the world to the next level.

These forms of currency have brought promise and hope to individuals worldwide; their promises embedded in words such as decentralization – the elimination of third parties such as banks from the transaction table –, low to zero transaction costs, high speed transactions and high security. Most people have only been made aware of the above strengths akin to the new technology.

However, a critique of this promises has yet to be done. If done, the critique would have raised one question: do these promises actually hold?

A look into the purchase of or transactions using Bitcoin paints a different picture as compared to the previously mentioned narrative. The picture is made dim by the realization that both purchasing Bitcoin and carrying out transactions is not entirely free. There exist both inherent as well as exogenous costs accruing to the user. As such, the question now shifts from whether transactions are free to how much do they actually cost? Furthermore, are they cheaper or more expensive as compared to the traditional banking system and if so, by how much?

Cryptocurrencies

This is not the case for Bitcoin alone. Other cryptocurrencies face similar challenges when trying to meet the expectations which the market has already hyped up. One such cryptocurrency is Monero, a top contender within the cryptocurrency market by market capitalization.

Monero presents a new realm to the cryptocurrency space – one discussed in the book – and is building on it to dominate the market. The latter has been the source of the coin's popularity among players within this space. However, not many people understand how it functions nor how it differs from other cryptocurrencies, especially Bitcoin. Moreover, with so many cryptocurrencies coming up in the market, the question on whether the difference is merely structural or one based on the ideology behind the formation of the coin and how this will influence the fulfilment of the promises made by the developers of the coin also lingers.

This book will answer the above questions and more.

The book will begin by shedding some light on cryptocurrencies and how they are expected to revolutionize the dynamics of global business. Here, the answer to the ever-so-debated question on the difference between digital money and cryptocurrencies will also be answered elaborately. It will, however, have an incline towards Bitcoin and Monero, trying to compare and contrast the two cryptocurrencies before finally detailing how users can benefit from their use in different settings. Eventually, a candid assessment of how the two are expected to fulfil their promises to the market will be given and its review done.

Over the course of this read, we will unravel the mystery surrounding cryptocurrencies, debunk its myths and provide in-depth information as to their future.

Real world examples

It is true that money has evolved over time.

The evolution of money dates back to a period before recorded history had taken root. However, the oldest recorded encounter between human beings and money occurs during the era of batter trade – a time when people exchanged goods for other goods which were deemed to be of the same value. However, the use of this form of money brought with it some complexities – such as the lack of double coincidence, indivisibility of some good, difficulty in making deferred payments and lack of an objective measure of value etc. – which in turn led to the formation of commodity money, metallic money, paper money, fiat money and plastic money.

The use of the above as money eventually raised a fundamental question: was money defined by its form or by its function – was it defined by the material of worth such as gold which was used as a medium of exchange or by the fact that that material was accepted as the medium of exchange?

Economists argued over the definition of money for a long time – specifically on whether it is defined by its form or function – and they eventually decided that the function of money as a medium of exchange was what gave money its significance. Its form, such as paper or metals, was merely meant to ensure the above role was achieved (this will be important when we get to cryptocurrencies).

Furthermore, over the course of the 20th century, the emergence of fiat money begun. This was a new form of currency which, rather than being backed by an item of value, was backed by the belief that a larger body was backing up the value of the paper of coin used in the exchange. In most cases, this form of money was backed by governments though initially banks and other such institutions – mostly large institutions – had some power in backing such currencies. For this form of money to be accepted, the people using it to trade had to believe in its value being as depicted on the coin or note – the most used forms of fiat money.

From the above, two main ideas arise: the fact that money was defined by its function rather than its form as well as the idea that the value of a currency was derived from the belief that the value on it was its actual value – this may or may not be backed by a financial institution or government. It is upon this backdrop that cryptocurrencies were formed.

Cryptocurrencies

Cryptography

Well, cryptocurrencies are the newest form of money in the market. By definition, cryptocurrencies are assets which are used as means of exchange – however, unlike other assets, they derive their name from the fact that they have their security as well as their functionality based on cryptography.

A rudimentary definition of the term would be that cryptography is the art of writing and solving codes. Without going into the technical details, the cryptography is based mainly on math and through it, other algorithms and protocols are enabled.

However, for readers with a more technical understanding of the term, cryptography has been synonymous with encryption –

techniques which are used to secure information from getting to third parties during communication – for the longest time. Encryption would convert sensible information into 'nonsense' with the help of computers. This was achieved through a process known as encoding – which was carried out by the computer which sent information – after which the recipient's computer would decode it.

The system since morphed and with the help of computational works, new forms of cryptography emerged. It was during this evolution period that the cryptographic hash function emerged.

The hash function is an exemplary way of encoding. It works through a simple principle, take in whatever data has been provided and put it in your own wording. As such, the data provided to the computer is converted into a series of fixed-size string of alphanumeric characters. This, for those with a rudimentary understanding, means that a word such as 'window' may be converted into an alphanumeric such as '43KI9CJ8'. The alphanumeric value defined above is known by many names: checksum (https://en.wikipedia.org/wiki/Checksum), digital fingerprint or merely hashes.

As such, this function converts data of any size using a hashing algorithm – known here as the hash function but described in detail later in this article – into output with a specific size (such as 256 bits).

These hash values are stored in tables. Therefore, when the computer goes through the different hash values, it then evaluates which text this hash was obtained from in a similar fashion as matching two similar characters on a table. As a result, it is a rule that no two texts, even if similar, should have the same cryptographic hash – known as cryptographic hash collisions – as a hacker may find the pattern and use it to evaluate the hash function used.

With this in mind, we can now work our way up to the system used by cryptocurrencies.

In cryptocurrencies, information from transactions in aggregated into blocks – this will be discussed in detail later in this text – and each block is assigned its own hash value. There exists a genesis block – the very first block that was formed – to which other blocks are tied. This block receives the first hash value in the chain. Thence, any block which is formed takes part of the hash value of its predecessor.

This being the case, all blocks formed after the genesis block will therefore have part of the hash from the genesis block. Furthermore, the content from this block cannot be altered given that alteration of this content would mean that even the hash functions would need to be altered – mainly because the content apportioned to that hash function has changed therefore the hash function cannot be mapped to this new content.

Upon this backdrop, in order to verify a transaction, computers on the decentralized network – nodes – would need to verify that the hash value from a specific block is tied to the hash value from its predecessor. If this is the case, then the blockchain network is stable. This very concept is what makes the entire blockchain network among the most secure networks available. This is because anyone wishing to change part of the block would need to alter the hash values of that block as well as that of all the blocks that succeed it. Furthermore, they need to do this while having higher computing power than the nodes within the network – as all nodes have to accept that this change has been made to a block. If the nodes have more computing power, they end up outperforming the attacker, eventually leading to the state prior to the hack. This makes nearly impossible – technically it is impossible – for a single hacker to change anything within the blockchain system.

However, this is not the only way cryptography works as digital signatures also play a role.

In simple terms, digital signatures are similar to handwritten signatures, as they prove that a certain individual actually carried out a transaction, except for the fact that they are held and operated on digitally. This is the case with web browsers which send digital signatures to the recipient's computers to verify that they are indeed from the authentic source.

For cryptocurrencies, these signatures come in two forms: public keys and private keys. These are sets of values which have an association with each other courtesy of some mathematical function. In most cases, these keys are 64-bit alphanumeric strings, similar to that of the hash.

Public keys ensure that people within the network can receive money or other information from the other players within the network. This key is available publicly. Private keys on the other hand aren't available publicly. This is because they are meant to ensure that the transaction emanates only from the account of the holder of the coins. This key is used to 'sign off' any transaction carried out by the user so as to ensure that the recipient can verify that the amount came from a specific user.

The signature from the keys doesn't change. Therefore, when the transactions are aggregated into a block, the signatures as well as the amounts tied to those signatures – courtesy of carrying out transactions – are assessed so as to ensure they do not change once that block is confirmed. This ensures transactions are recorded as are.

All in all, cryptocurrencies have found their grounding within cryptography. The technology (cryptocurrencies) have become synonymous with hashing and digital signatures with good reason. However, these are only the basis on which the technology works. The real technology on which cryptocurrencies are based is known as the blockchain.

The Blockchain System

The entire cryptocurrency system works on the blockchain platform. This platform is a decentralized and distributed ledger[1] system in which the transactions that occur within a specific period are recorded and bundled up into a block[2] and recorded.

The notion of decentralization stems from the fact that there is no

---

[1] A ledger is a book (traditionally) or system in which transactions are recorded and stored in order for the accountants to refer to when consolidating accounts or for auditors to refer to during audits.

[2] A block is a group of transactions which have been bundled together.

Cryptocurrencies

single body which governs the transactions carried out on the network (which is unlike modern transactions which are governed by banks or service providers such as Visa). This, according to the founder of this system – Satoshi Nakamoto – was meant to ensure that the power of transactions was given back to the people rather than to huge corporations which stand to benefit greatly from holding people's money.

Moreover, the distributed ledger stems from the fact that once transactions are validated, the blocks are shared with all the nodes within the system. This ensures that all the nodes store the blockchain data such that there is not a single computer that is said to be the store of all the information. This goes a long way in furthering the concept of decentralization.

The system works on the principle that information contained within a block cannot be altered and that the block is assigned a hash value linked to that of its predecessor. in order for transactions to be recorded, the entire network of nodes – computers around the globe connected to a network which validates the cryptographic hash – need to decipher the cryptographic hash and move on to decipher the next block. A transaction is considered authentic when the nodes move to decipher the next block, at which point that block is stored within the blockchain.

The system is also programmed to read the longest chain as the correct one. Therefore, given that the entire chain of blocks stems from the genesis block and has part of the harsh from this block, generally the nodes will read this chain as the correct chain. Any additions to the blockchain will generally be added on to the longest chain and all the nodes will receive the new blocks to their systems upon their approval. This also explains why cryptocurrencies are said to be decentralized – courtesy of the nodes – while also explaining how the security of the entire blockchain is ensured – attackers need to have higher computing power to form a chain other than the longest one and get it accepted by the entire network.

However, questions arise: how do we therefore maintain the stability of the network or compensate the owners for all the nodes for keeping the network stable?

To answer the first question, the nodes are compensated based on a proof of work mechanism.

Proof of work is a mechanism/concept which was first designed to operate for Bitcoin. Its designer – Satoshi Nakamoto – meant it to be the forerunner to a decentralized economy with peer to peer payment systems.

The proof of work concept is one where the nodes have to continuously 'work' to solve the cryptographic hash problem. In this case, the work means that the nodes, having been pre-installed with the cryptocurrency's program, need to keep solving for the cryptographic hash problem for all new blocks generated. With an average of one block being generated per 10 minutes or about 144 blocks per day, the nodes need to ensure that each of these blocks is both solved for and added to the longest chain. This means that every time the nodes are working towards both ensuring that the blocks which are generated are added to the system with complete and accurate transactions and in the process ensure that the entire system is secure.

Over time, especially due to the exponential increase in the number of coins released, the mining process becomes harder. Numerically, with every 2,016 blocks created, the difficulty level required in mining is adjusted. This adjustment is based on several factors: the number of blocks mined, the number of nodes which took part in the mining process and the time taken to hash the 2,016 blocks. Over time, the difficulty level for most cryptocurrencies has been increasing as more and more miners get into the network.

This has led to more powerful systems being used to carry out mining. Initially, all that was needed was a CPU (Central Processing Unit), however, this transformed to GPUs (Graphics Processing Units) then to FPGAs (Field-Programmable Gate Arrays). Eventually, mining specific computers known as ASICs (Application-Specific Integrated Circuits) were created in order to ensure that miners had sufficient power to carry out mining effectively. Their creation made the previous three hardware options obsolete unless they were pooled together in a group.

These machines, however, have a major drawback. In order to mine, the electricity costs incurred are quite high. It is estimated that the cost of electricity attributable to mining cryptocurrencies – specifically Bitcoin – stands at about $5,000 per coin or approximately $200 per day. With such high costs seen within the network, miners require to make higher margins to offset these costs, a factor which brings us to our next question: how are node owners compensated for keeping the network stable?

In a bid to ensure decentralization is effective, the nodes within the network receive some compensation for their role of securing the network. This compensation comes in form of coins which are released to the network upon the completion of specific tasks – these tasks mainly entail the deciphering of a certain number of blocks within the network: once these blocks have been deciphered, the owners are compensated. Given this, the owners of the computers within this chain are referred to as miners.

For miners, the additional coin is meant to offset for their loss in money courtesy of electricity costs. Given the high amount of electricity consumed during the mining process, the miners use the coins received as a payoff for the high costs incurred in both the acquisition of the machinery used in mining as well as the resources used in the mining process, key being electricity.

The number of coins released, however, has slowly been reducing over time. Initially, the compensation stood at 50 coins for the first 210,000 blocks formed and this number keeps halving every time the number of blocks double. This, coupled with the fact that the number of miners has increased significantly over time, means that each coin released to the market now has to be split between the miners based on their computational power – hashing power – which makes the reward much smaller for new entrants than it was for their forerunners. However, given that the value of the coins in also increasing during this period, the gains made from its increased value may offset the small size of reward currently being received.

With all the above intricacies akin to cryptocurrencies, they seem to be a significant leap into the future of payments. With the 'entire world' being part of the validation process and the transactions being limited to peer to peer, there is a lot to benefit from when using them as a payment mechanism. Furthermore, the fact that the payments are available via a digital front makes it more convenient using cryptocurrencies.

Digital Currencies Versus Cryptocurrencies

Based on the above, it would be fair to conclude that cryptocurrencies can be said to be digital currencies – given the space they operate within. However, do the two have the same meaning? Can one be equivocated for the other?

The answer is no.

While it is true that cryptocurrencies are digital currencies, not all digital currencies are cryptocurrencies. By definition, digital currencies are forms of money which exist only in digital form – thus making cryptocurrencies digital currencies – however, such currency maintains the characteristics of fiat money. The main difference between digital currency and fiat money is the state in which it is held (cash versus electronic). Mostly, digital currencies are held through service providers such as PayPal, Skrill and Google Wallet and these services are enabled by the internet.

In contrast, cryptocurrencies derive their name from the fact that they are based on cryptography and operate based on this system. These currencies, however, operate on the digital space, making them all digital currencies despite there being some contrasts.

Unlike cryptocurrency, digital currency does not have a decentralized system backing the flow of funds. Rather, the system is manned by a centralized body – mostly a company – and the funds are deemed to be secure based on the security protocols that the body puts in place. Furthermore, the peer to peer element does not exist as money sent from one person to the next has to go through the service provider – for the transaction cost to be calculated and deducted – before it gets to the recipient.

While this payment method (PayPal) may take a much shorter period to be completed as compared to cryptocurrencies, the transaction costs may lead to more people preferring cryptocurrencies over PayPal. With the advancement in cryptocurrencies – such as the implementation of the Segregated Witness protocol and lightning networks, transactions will end up being much faster and this will necessitate a shift from digital currencies to cryptocurrencies. This shift, we expect, will be driven by the appreciation of the blockchain technology by the general public, a move which will propel the world to the next currency phase.

The advancements in money, as seen above, have been quite significant. With the world moving forward at a high rate, we decided to take a look at how two cryptocurrencies are driving this agenda across the globe.

Bitcoin

Introduction

The evolution of money did not stop with fiat money. Everyday more and more people device ways to make money serve its purpose as a method of exchange. This process has been characterized by tremendous hurdles especially from central governments which believe they will lose control of the financial system – which is their tool of enforcing monetary policy within the economy. However, the fact that money draws its value from its acceptance by the community has come to overshadow these hurdles.

Cryptocurrencies are the breakthrough which exemplified this and their forerunner, Bitcoin, became the excellent exemplar. Through this system, a shift in modern economics is about to be driven. Over the next section of this book, we will evaluate how this is the case as well as the benefits that will accrue the holders of this cryptocurrency moving forward.

History of Bitcoin

The history of Bitcoin is the history of cryptocurrency. It can be traced back to a document which was published in 2008 by an anonymous developer only known by their pseudo name: Satoshi Nakamoto – shortly after the global financial crisis.

The above was driven by the realization that the management in the top financial institutions, during the financial crisis period, suffered from moral hazard[3] and this led to institutions greatly risking funds belonging to individuals thus affecting their livelihoods adversely upon the stock market collapse. Therefore, this new system provided a new means to remove the power from financial institutions and place it back to the owners of the money. This also had the added benefit of cutting transaction costs associated with having an intermediary down to zero or near zero.

The paper in question was titled 'Bitcoin: The Peer-to-Peer Electronic Cash System'.

In it was information on a new form of exchange system that utilized the computational power of different computers across the globe to bring together a cash exchange system that would effectively eliminate intermediaries. This system harnessed the power of new technology dubbed 'blockchain'. Blockchain was to be a revolution to the financial industry. As earlier defined, a block is a set of transactions that have been grouped together. Based on the latter, a blockchain is therefore a chain of blocks.

The Decentralized and Distributed Network

The design of the blockchain system places more weight on the longest chain – given that this chain is most likely the most accepted chain. Therefore, as more blocks are formed, the longer the blockchain gets and effectively, the more secure the network is[4].

---

[3] The principal/agent problem whereby the agent acts in a manner only to serve their own interests (such as taking up high risk using the agent's money without assessing its implications on the agent) especially in a situation where they presume themselves 'insured' by the fact that they can be bailed out by a larger body such as a government.

Satoshi made it such that in order for a player to become a node within the chain, they needed to download the entire system onto their computers. Once you had it, every node received a copy of the accepted blocks onto their computer – which gave the system its name as a distributed ledger. The above, coupled with the fact that the blockchain system was decentralized – not governed by a single body or institution – meant that all players within the network had access to the financial transactions from the network.

This has been the reason behind the network's growth from about 876 megabytes in the first quarter of 2012 to its current size of over 149 gigabytes.

The Mining Architecture

Satoshi's concept of a proof of work system is in itself a brilliant idea deduced from the basic concept of money: as more and more people accept it as a means of exchange, the more it meets its role and being this means of exchange. Satoshi's expectation was that this would hold for Bitcoin (as well as for other cryptocurrencies which came after it) since its popularity among people – especially during the time of the global financial crisis – would rise quite fast and this dream came fruition soon after.

---

[4] This is based on the initial paper whereby Satoshi wrote that as the network grew, it would require that the computational power of the hacker be higher than that of the whole network for them to hack it. For a much larger network, the probability of this fell exponentially with each new block thus effectively making the blockchain a secure network in itself.

History

To enforce this, Satoshi used an already elaborate program: the secure hashing algorithm (SHA).

The secure hashing algorithm was created by the United States National Security Agency (NSA). It was designed to be a set of cryptographic hash functions based initially on Merkle–Damgård structure. Initially, the NSA had built a SHA-1 algorithm – which was the forerunner to all such algorithms – but the quick advancements within this field led to more complex and dynamic algorithms being developed leading to the development of the SHA-2. From this algorithm came the SHA-224, SHA-256, SHA-384, SHA-512 and others.

The transition was attributable to a key characteristic of hashing – hashes were meant follow the no collision attribute. Given that secure hashing algorithms are designed to ensure security, any vulnerability to this system – especially one pertaining the collision attribute – needed to be assessed. As such, both algorithms were tested for this.

Based on this, it was concluded that collision – previously defined as the ability for two inputs to generate the same hash – was possible for any hashing algorithm, however, the probability of collision differed between different algorithms. Upon testing, the results showed that the SHA-1 algorithm was more prone to collision unlike the SHA-2.

This vulnerability played a key role in the removal of the SHA-1 algorithm from key web browsers back in January 2017 and paved the way for the entry of SHA-2 into the market. Since then, SHA-2 has become the gold standard within the cryptography field and has come to support major corporations in their endeavour to encode their clients' credentials.

Bitcoin and SHA-2

With such trust having been placed in the SHA-2 hashing algorithm, it came as no surprise when Satoshi selected the SHA-256 as the algorithm of choice. Users of the Bitcoin system were meant to download the package and run this algorithm on the different blocks which were created. The hashing algorithm was tailored in a way to ensure that a unique hash was created for every block, however, due to its structure, newer blocks could have part of the characteristics of the previous hash.

In the case of Bitcoin, the transactions would be bundled together every 10 minutes – meaning that during this period, at least one block will be fully hashed and a coin mined – and a hash tried on the block over and over until a unique hash specific to the bock was developed. However, in cases where this block would not have completed the hashing process, then an adjustment was made to it so as to ensure its complete hashing actually took place.

Given that this hash is tailored to the entire block, the idea as to how the different transactions within the block are maintained by the system often comes to question. To answer it, it is important to understand a different structure: the Merkle tree structure.

The Merkle tree brings a new twist to the hashing process. The ideology of the tree stems from the fact that the different transactions within the block – leaves – are themselves hashed and that the eventual result is the final hash resulting from both the transactions' hashes as well as the entire block's hashes – the root. This system ensures that all the transactions within the chain are maintained safely within the block. With this system in place, the only way for an attacker to change a transaction in the system would be for them to complete a hash of all transactions within that block as well as all which succeeded that block while at the same time maintaining a higher computational power than the system's users. This is impractical in reality and, as earlier stated, is the reason why Bitcoin is regarded safe within itself.

Bitcoin Mining: Difficulty

The mining of Bitcoin was initially designed to be done using the power from the central processing units (CPUs). In the earlier days, there were few people mining the cryptocurrency while at the same time only few transactions taking place during the period. As such, the hashing power which was required to run the network was quite minimal.

Over time, however, both the network users – leading to a higher number of transactions using Bitcoin – and number of miners grew. This is exemplified by the fact that the number of Bitcoin wallets kept growing over time, rising from just over 3.17 million back in the first quarter of 2015 to the over 21.5 million user wallets which were recorded in the fourth quarter of 2017. This led to the number of transactions during these periods rising from just over 85,000 transactions per day to nearly 200,000 transactions per day over the first quarter of 2015 to the fourth quarter of 2017 respectively.

Furthermore, the number of miners also rose during this period from the under 5,000 miners recorded back in 2013 to the over 100,000 recorded in 2017 – with the expected number of miners rising as the price of Bitcoin rises. This alluded to an increasing demand for the cryptocurrency both for the purpose of transactions as well as from the miners.

Such an increase in the number of miners, though welcome by the system as a way to enhance its security through an increase in the nodes, led to increased competition within the network. Over time, it became clearer that Central Processing Units (CPUs) were becoming obsolete in this mining process, leading to the shift towards Graphical Processing Units (GPUs). These complex processors were mainly used within the gaming world where faster processing power was required for rendering purposes. However, as with CPUs, the use of GPUs for mining purposes was quickly replaced by FPGAs (Field-Programmable Gate Arrays) and finally by ASICs (Application-Specific Integrated Circuits).

The entry of each new technology to the system was pivotal to the increased difficulty in the system's hashing. This figure which is computed using the tera hashes per second (TH/s) – easier defined as trillions of hashes per second – has been rising constantly through the years.

As at 2013 (during the period where CPUs completed the hashing process), the figure stood at 21 TH/s and rose to nearly 80,000 TH/s in mid-2014 (during the period where GPUs completed the hashing process). As at the end of January 2018, the figure had skyrocketed to over 21.6 million TH/s, a factor which alludes to the difficulty which has been brought about by the entry of Application-Specific

Integrated Circuits into the mining space.

With the exponential increase in the hashing power required by the system came a new factor: the costs of mining kept rising. The key driver of this cost was the electricity costs which miners had to incur. This cost would further be exacerbated by the high price of purchasing Application-Specific Integrated Circuits. Miners therefore needed to be compensated for their role in keeping the system in its safe state and this led Satoshi to come up with a reward system.

Bitcoin Mining: Payoff

The difficulty in the hash rate was not the only problem that rocked cryptocurrency miners as they were also faced with a reducing Bitcoin reward for their mining role. Satoshi set up the reward algorithm in a manner that postulated that with the increase in the number of blocks released into the market – therefore the number of coins released – came the increase in difficulty in obtaining the cryptocurrency.

The reward scheme was set up in such a way initially, 50 Bitcoins would be distributed to the network with each block that was accepted. This meant that early adopters of the cryptocurrency benefited from having a higher reward for their work. However, this reward was meant to keep reducing over time. Over the first 210,000 blocks, it would be maintained at 50 Bitcoins per block but this figure would keep falling by half for every new 210,000 blocks – therefore between 210,000 blocks and 420,000 blocks the number of Bitcoins produced per block would reduce to 25 and reduce further to 12.5 between 420,000 blocks and 630,000 blocks and so on.

This payoff mechanism was meant to ensure that the cap for Bitcoins would be held at 21 million. As such, the number of Bitcoins released to the system would fall by a reducing balance over time. As at February 2018, the figure stood at 12.5 Bitcoins per block and is expected to half later in 2021.

Going forward, Satoshi also accounted for the fact that given the number of Bitcoins was had a cap, once all Bitcoins were distributed, it would be impossible for miners to benefit from the rising value of the coin. As such, they came up with an elaborate measure for this whereby the miners would be apportioned a percentage of the fees associated with carrying out transactions using the Bitcoin system. Given that the transactions were also on the rise, it was clear that the miners would need this system in future.

Bitcoin and Privacy

The growing size of the blockchain and the increased network size, despite having their perks, ended up having its downside. The main among this was on the reduced bandwidth within the network – as each node is doing a similar thing with the others – thus leading to a bottleneck in the network's scalability.

Bitcoin, courtesy of the above, would take a long period to accept, record and complete the transaction as it had to be accepted by the network as well as go through different roll-back problems that need to take shape. As such, after taking about 10 minutes to accept the transaction, it would take longer for it to reflect in the recipient's wallet, making scalability a problem. Despite this being a problem, the time taken was still shorter than it took for other traditional methods such as cheques which took about 2 days to clear.

Over time, courtesy of its advantages as well as its first mover advantage, Bitcoin has come to be accepted as a payment mechanism by many of its holders. This, however, has not stopped developers from noticing certain drawbacks akin to Bitcoin and working towards solving them.

One of these drawbacks is in anonymity (discussed later) and this is where Monero comes in.

Monero

Introduction

The evolution of cryptocurrencies has come a long way and with it has come a proliferation in the number of cryptocurrencies. Over the year ended December 2017, there was a surge in the number of Initial Coin Offerings (ICOs) in the market with the number rising from about 50 in 2016 to over 200 during the 2017 period.

Over time, it has become clearer to developers that they needed to differentiate themselves from other players within the market. Therefore, developers have decided to find different ways of creating their own niche within this space. This has led to different cryptocurrencies being formed in a bid to solve different global problems. Currently, cryptocurrencies have been tailored towards solving specific problems with cryptocurrencies being developed to solve education sector flaws, energy sector flaws and so on. Moreover, other have been tailored towards solving some of the problems akin to the initial blockchain architecture such as scalability, security or privacy. Such coins are tailored towards specific problems and their solutions developed to solve for them.

An exemplar of such a coin is Monero, a rising cryptocurrency which was developed to cater to cryptocurrency users who had one need, privacy.

History

Monero's history dates back to 18th April 2014 when the coin was launched to the Bitcoin talk platform by a person with the pseudonym 'thankful_for_today'. Back then, its name was

BitMonero, a name which would later change to Monero about five days later. Prior to this, however, it is said that the underlying protocol on which it is based – the CryptoNote protocol – was originally launched by an author by the pseudonym Nicolas van Saberhagen.

During its creation, developers had one idea in mind: the promotion of privacy. This coin, unlike other cryptocurrencies, was developed with the sole interest of ensuring that it served a segment within the business community that did not wish to have their records go public. This included institutions such as banks as well as other financial institutions which have a duty of confidentiality to their clients or other private corporations which are not mandated to store their records publicly and prefer to keep these records private.

The talk on privacy was, however, both its strong suit and its detriment.

The coin's acceptance grew quickly courtesy of its applicability within the dark web – a section of the web which is uncontrolled and in which criminals easily find access to some of their weapons as well as other immoral services (thus dark web) and can only be accessed through specific web applications. As early as 2016, only two years after its launch, the cryptocurrency was being used by AlphaBay, a market within the dark web community. Shortly after the realization, the site was closed by law enforcement.

It is postulated by some that the reason behind the rise of Monero was its favouritism by illegal traders and criminals who preferred to remain anonymous during such trades or activities (as shown by its increased used within the AlphaBay network). However, the cryptocurrency builds its own case by stating that the good from its use within financial and other private institutions by far outweighs the bad that is presented to the world on the demerits of the cryptocurrency.

While building on its name and its key attribute, the cryptocurrency has grown to become one of the largest in the market – based on market capitalization statistics – and stands at twelfth position as at February 2018.

Developmental Cornerstones

Monero was formed on four key pillars: privacy, security, intractability and fungibility. All these (except security), according to the developers, were meant to be additions to the already existing cryptocurrency frameworks such as decentralization, scalability and proof-of-work, all which the cryptocurrency meets. As stated, given that Monero used a similar framework as did Bitcoin, the same security options akin to other blockchain users were available for them.

However, it is when we get to the other pillars that we establish the benefits of Monero.

Ring Signatures

First in on privacy where Monero went ahead to bring to the market a novel idea, the ring signatures.

This novel technology was developed by Ron Rivest, Adi Shamir, and Yael Tauman back in 2001 in a bid to counter the negative implications of the lack of privacy which surrounded cryptographic algorithms back then. Advancements to this initial idea were then made by Fujisaki and Suzuki and these formed the basis for the new ring signatures system.

Ring signatures are established by mixing the keys – private or public – from different transactions within a group thus ensuring that individuals outside of these transactions cannot identify the initiator or recipient of the funds from a specific transaction. The architecture of this system was the basis on which the name ring signatures was formed as it was designed in such a way that the keys of the initiator or recipient were mixed in a ring-like fashion (given that they were in a group). This, tied with the fact that real identities are obscured via blockchain technology, means that the transactions are in turn untraceable – a factor which made Monero seem like a safe haven for criminals.

These two differ significantly from Bitcoin and other cryptocurrencies which stocks to the address provided so as to transfer the funds from one account to another and despite there being no link between the account holder and their address, individuals can track back a specific set of transactions meticulously back to a specific individual once their address comes to light.

At this time, however, Monero's developers had been made aware of the coin's reputation as being a black-market coin, one meant to ensure the security of criminals. They therefore made adjustments to their platform.

Spend and View Keys

Monero is termed by many as being opaquely-transparent. Given that most of Monero's users were institutions or individuals operating legally within their respective countries, it was only a matter of time before the government or other regulatory bodies begun looking into some of their documents. With Monero being an opaque cryptocurrency, such an exercise would have been deemed impossible, a factor which would have been detrimental for the cryptocurrency.

As such, the developers coined a way in which the cryptocurrency's transparency would be achieved. This was through the issuance of a spend and view key.

The spend key, the users can spend. It was quite similar to any other cryptocurrency key as its role was to ensure that the user could conduct their transactions as is the case for all cryptocurrencies. However, it was in the next key that transparency was achieved.

The view key allowed the users to allow other parties to view the transactions which they take part. It serves as some type of access for authorized users only into an individual's transactional history on Monero. Through this, the user is in total control of their account and can decide when they wish to take whichever action. This is especially beneficial for financial institutions which can use the view key to provide access to auditors or regulators during audit periods or tax filing periods respectively

Fungibility

Finally came fungibility – the ability of one coin to be equivocated for another with the same value as itself.

To give this some context, Bitcoin has its coins tied to the addresses which they have gone through. Due to this, once these coins have moved from one account to the next, they store the codes for the accounts through which they moved. As such, an individual can decide not to accept coins from certain accounts such as those which have been seen to conduct illegal trades or crime – this is not necessarily a bad thing as it may alleviate such crimes, however, if the previous owner of the coin had no knowledge that their coin had been used for such activities, this places them at a disadvantage.

Fungibility comes to solve for this by ensuring that any trader can accept any coins as their value is similar. As such, these coins can be equivocated for each other and, as a result of the coins' lack of traceability, no one can pinpoint a single coin as is the case with Bitcoin.

Mining Architecture

All the above developments have driven Monero to its success. The coin has solved quite a number of problems akin to the cryptocurrency space in its own fashion. Currently, its developers seem to have clearly cut out their niche and focused their efforts at satisfying their customers.

Despite this being so, it is also important to cater to the needs of the individuals keeping the system safe. In this section, we thus look at Monero's mining process.

History

Satoshi's initial goal was for there to be an elaborate 'one-CPU-one-vote' system in cryptocurrencies. Such a system would ensure that all nodes within the system had equal rights in governing the system and this would ensure that the entire system was fully decentralized. However, this was curtailed by the emergence of more sophisticated machines such as Application-Specific Integrated Circuits.

Such machines brought about competition with the then popular Central Processing Unit mining method. With their processing power being unequalled, miners had to gather resources and purchase the expensive equipment in order to profitably continue with the mining process. This in turn was against the very goal set out by Satoshi as individuals with more resources had more power than those with less. This meant that if individuals with resources purchased more of the ASICs, they would then have more power to govern the system.

Developers at Monero realized this significant flaw within the Bitcoin architecture and implemented a solution to it, the CryptoNote protocol.

CryptoNote

The CryptoNote protocol came to provide the solution to this problem.

Similar to the SHA-256 algorithm which is present in most cryptocurrencies, CryptoNote employs a proof-of-work system whereby nodes within the system have to take part in the hashing process for the reward-based system to hold. However, that is as far as their similarities go.

CryptoNote then diverges into ensuring some form of equity among miners by employing a memory bound function. This function bases the time to a solution on the amount of memory deemed necessary for that specific problem to be solved. This is unlike the CPU bound function whereby the processing power is the variable assessed in determining the time necessary to complete the hashing process.

The use of the memory bound function removes the use of processors with higher computing power – courtesy of the pipeline[5] effect – from the equation. As a result, machines using pipelined systems are eliminated from this, leaving only Central Processing Units – x86 and upwards – and Graphics Processing Units in the mining space.

Through this, the system solved one of the major flaws with many cryptocurrency mining systems and gave miners a level playing field on which to operate. CryptoNote therefore served as a major plus to miners.

---

[5] The pipeline effect (instruction pipelining) occurs when instructions sent to a processor are divided into smaller sequential steps from which the processor can execute them. This means that the processor can, instead of completing a transaction as a whole then moving to the next transaction, execute bits of instructions in parallel therefore allowing it to complete more instructions much quicker and in a much more efficient manner. This, however, has a negative effect on the response time of the software (increases latency).

The Battle of the Cryptocurrencies

Behind the Battle

The previous chapters have spoken to all the benefits and drawbacks of the two cryptocurrencies. It is clear that they (cryptocurrencies) have brought to the world great solutions not only their form but also in how they operate. These currencies have brought with them a revolution to the modern economics age by both changing the dynamics of most economics concept – as we will see in the use of cryptocurrencies as a store of value later in this book – as well as integrating currencies with technology. This presents a new age to users of money as well as its regulators as Central Banks are now being made more aware of this development and its role in the world.

This being said, these cryptocurrencies have also been seen to be dynamic in the solutions they have brought to the market. Starting with their forerunner, Bitcoin, these currencies have been built on different systems. The diversity in their architecture is also palpable and people attribute this to the different solutions they bring to the market. These differences have both their positives and drawbacks – as this concept is still in its development stage and still undergoing major transformations – but on the overall, they are a step in the positive direction.

Despite this, it is important to critique some of these differences so as to address especially the drawbacks to the system. Here, we the two coins are assessed based on their characteristics and the solutions to some of their drawbacks given.

Bitcoin Versus Monero

It is important to start by stating that both coins have one fundamental role, to act as a medium of exchange. Over time, it is becoming increasingly clear both to governments and to their citizens that cryptocurrencies are playing this role as effectively as was the case in the traditional system.

However, it is in playing this role that we find the first drawback to the two cryptocurrencies.

Scalability

Both cryptocurrencies are quite slow in their transaction times. It takes over 20 minutes for both of the cryptocurrencies to reflect that a transaction has been undertaken in the system, a factor which would have negative effects on business worldwide.

The current business environment has been based on the fast and efficient systems of service providers. This is clear to any user who has used the services of companies such as Visa or Mastercard as these companies' complete transactions over a period of seconds. Users merely need to swipe their card and are sure that the receiver will receive the money shortly after and this has made business around the globe much faster.

This explains why users having to wait over 30 minutes for a transaction to be verified by a system would be setting the world of business back by over a decade. Both coins are therefore poorer at accomplishing this role than the traditional system. Let us understand how.

Bitcoin's system takes about 10 minutes to mine a coin, meaning that a block is created every ten minutes. Given that every transaction is recorded in the ledger after the block has been mined, it would take about 10 minutes for a single transaction to be recorded on the ledger. However, it does not end here as the wallet must show that this transaction has been completed and this is where it takes time.

It takes another thirty to forty-five minutes after the first ten minutes for a transaction to be deemed complete at which period the confirmation to the wallets of the recipient of the coin receive the notice of completion of this transaction. in short, Bitcoin users need to wait in a line at a grocery store for forty-five minutes for their payment to reflect in the store's system before they can leave during which period a credit card user has already made a meal back home.

This is not the case for Bitcoin alone as Monero in turn takes nearly four minutes for a transaction to be recorded and about 26 minutes for confirmations to be sent on the different wallets.

The two situations above stem from one problem which affects all cryptocurrencies: scalability[6]. Given that the transaction processing capacity of the cryptocurrency network is limited by the average block creation time – which stands at about 10 minutes for Bitcoin and just over two minutes for Monero – and the block sizes are

---

[6] The scalability problem refers to the limits on the amount of transactions the cryptocurrency network can process. It is a consequence of the fact that records (known as blocks) in theblockchainare limited in size and frequency.These blocks include the transactions on the cryptocurrency network.

limited, the network's throughput is generally limited. Therefore, the transaction processing capacity is limited to a specific number of transactions per unit time.

The scalability problem is one which affects the above cryptocurrencies significantly and one which, despite the benefits of the blockchain network, has led to individuals and entities not accepting these cryptocurrencies. With players such as fast food networks receiving millions in revenue from the thousands of transactions daily, it would be hard to verify these transactions hours after they occurred.

As such, despite Monero being a much better cryptocurrency on this segment – based on the higher transaction speed – both of these cryptocurrencies need to do a lot before they receive the acceptance that service providers such as Visa receive.

Privacy

As previously alluded to, Monero was created so as to overcome one key drawback of Bitcoin: its lack of privacy.

Through the use of ring signatures and fungibility, Monero has ensured that neither can a user's address be viewed or tracked by another user on the platform and that the amounts transferred by a user can also not be tracked by others. This solves a recurring problem with Bitcoin whereby users can refuse to accept coins tied to certain accounts – mostly accounts with ties to criminal activity.

This keenness to privacy has brought about Monero's fondness among certain players within the cryptocurrency space. It is expected to play a major role in the future of Monero.

The Better Coin

With the above in mind, it is quite visible that Monero came to solve for the drawbacks of Bitcoin. The discussion on which of the two reigns superior has yet to be exhausted as these boils down mostly to preference.

Despite there seeming to be an objective way to review cryptocurrencies, most individuals simply choose Monero due to their preference for anonymity. However, if analysed, among the key things to look at would be the coin's acceptability (as shown by the size of their user base), how many coins are already distributed[7], the team behind its development as well as the market it is targeting.

On all of the above, both coins perform quite well despite Bitcoin overshadowing Monero in terms of its acceptability. However, it is also important to acknowledge that both cryptocurrencies bring a lot to the table and that their functionality is beneficial to the financial community.

---

[7] The number of distributed coins gives one an idea on how large a share price surge would affect the coin. Coins with much lower distribution end up benefiting from having a lower supply therefore a much larger demand and finally a much higher price in contrast to those with a much higher distribution.

How to buy?

The above cryptocurrencies are mostly purchased through different exchanges. An advantage they have is that due to their large market capitalization therefore reputation within the market, it is easy to purchase them unlike other smaller alt coins.

Bitcoin has the advantage of being available on every exchange across the globe. However, the easiest platforms to buy it are Coinbase and CoinMama. Coinbase especially was formed back in 2011 by two developers, Brian Armstrong and Fred Ehrsam after which it quickly grew into one of the largest exchanges in the world. Currently, it operates in over 32 countries in the world and has morphed to incorporate a cryptocurrency application in the process. To run an account, one needs to register on the site with authentic identification documents and in order to trade, there are fees which must be paid.

The site has currently incorporated a vault which is a safe place to store one's coins. Through this, it is trying to ensure that they beef up security on their platform. The platform ensures that one can sign up either as an individual or as a group after which they receive services such as a 48-hour withdrawal period from which they can cancel the withdrawal and group authentication, all in a bid to boost security.

For Monero, there are only but a few exchanges that allow it to be traded. These exchanges include Poloniex, Bittrex, Shapeshift, Bitfinex and Changelly.

Of all the above, Shapeshift is the one exchange that does not require the user to include their details, rather, they merely need to include the account they are transferring their coins from or to.

With its fees differing between cryptocurrencies, it serves as one of the best platforms for individuals to obtain different cryptocurrencies without having to register. Furthermore, of all the exchanges detailed, it is the one exchange which operates across the globe – with the exception of North Korea and New York (due to the Bitfinex laws within the state).

With this, we presume that investors will find it easy to invest in either of the above cryptocurrencies and benefit from these investments courtesy of a high return on them.

JOHAN VON AMSTERDAM

Storing Cryptocurrencies

Underlying Economics

Money serves different functions in the human life. Primarily, it is used as a measure of payment therefore used in facilitating trade between different parties. Over time, however, the functions of money kept evolving and other roles were added on.

One key role courtesy of this morphosis was the role of money as a store of wealth. People begun using money as an asset, one which would be held for long period and used to store the value the money had over long periods. Innately, money acted in the same capacity as shares or commodities since people could now hold it for longer periods. This role was driven by a different economic factor: interest[8] rates.

However, there was one fear inherent in this function: people could only hold money as a store of value if the inflation[9] rate in the economy was low. If this rate kept rising, money holders were seen

---

[8] Interest rate is the amount of return one earns on saving their money rather than using it for consumption – the technical explanation for this is that interest rates serve as a return to compensate the holder of money for foregoing current consumption for future consumption.

[9] Inflation is a term used in economics to define the deterioration in the purchasing power of money. It is computed by assessing the amount of goods an individual could buy at a certain historical period in time versus how much they can buy at present. On the overall, economists believe that a little inflation is necessary in an economy as it acts as an incentive for producers to keep producing goods or rendering services, however, once inflation rises above set targets, it begins to have negative implications on the economy, especially on poor people who cannot afford the now expensive gods.

to be losing value as their money could only buy a little amount of goods at that period as compared to what it could previously buy. This was mainly because during periods of high inflation the interest rate earned from saving money is way lower than the loss in the value of money courtesy of the high inflation, necessitating people to consume more. Given this, individuals needed to be kept in the know on the inflation rates in a country and with the evolution of governments and Central Banks, this became a key concern for them as the realization that it tied to other economic factors became clearer.

In their formation, cryptocurrencies factored in the above economic characteristics of money and made significant changes to them. First, the finite nature of cryptocurrencies would see their value rise over time, meaning that the holders of these currencies were being compensated for holding them through time.

Interest rates are therefore taken out of the equation as individuals holding these cryptocurrencies is innately self-paying. Moreover, once an individual received a loan using cryptocurrencies, the interest they paid out on them would keep rising over time, leading the loan to become unpayable. On to inflation, cryptocurrencies have come up with fixed inflation rates governing the entire system. These rates are based on how many cryptocurrencies are released to the world over a particular period of time. Developers have made it a priority to limit this number so as to ensure that people benefit from low inflation.

This clearly shows the ideology behind holding cryptocurrencies: consistency in purchasing power. As such, holding cryptocurrencies will, in future, be driven primarily by the need to gain from their rising value. Their finite nature acts as a demand-driver, ensuring that individuals continuously benefit from a system which does not merely hurt the poor – due to the high inflation rates (as well as hyper-inflation in some cases) which characterized the old system – while making the rich richer – due to the high interest rates the rich received during periods of high inflation.

Despite all this, cryptocurrencies faced one key hurdle: how could a digital currency which was new to the market and decentralized be stored? At this time, these currencies were prone to hacking from attackers and this only became worse after their increase in value was seen by the market. Such attacks necessitated developers to come together and develop more secure methods of storing these currencies. These methods are discussed in the next section.

The Store of Value: Cryptocurrency Wallets

Cryptocurrency wallets can be broken down into five: desktop wallets, online wallets, hardware wallets, paper wallets and mobile wallets. As with the name, these wallets are operated on the different platforms encompassed in the name therein.

Desktop wallets were the first type of wallets created with their forerunner, Bitcoin Core, being the first of this kind. Back then, these wallets were made to serve the purpose of storage only. However, with time, their purpose was augmented to suit different clientele such as those who preferred advanced security or anonymity got to get their own different wallets. Such include Armory and Electrum.

With time, however, convenience came into play as people needed to have their wallets with them more often so as to allow for them to pay for some of their goods and services while on the road, leading to the creation of mobile wallets. These wallets were meant to purely support payments using this cryptocurrency. Unlike other full bitcoin clients – who had to download the entire blockchain framework – these run on a portion of this framework and have the notion of simplified payment verification behind their formation.

The online wallet came by default courtesy of Bitcoin being a digital currency. They provided online service to clients with their personal information being stored on a company's server. However, this was in turn a drawback, the cryptocurrencies were meant to give the control to the holder and not to an entity storing the holder's information. Be though this the case, they have served the purpose of ensuring people are connected to the cryptocurrency space. Such platforms include sites like Coinbase or Blockchain.info.

The next two wallets came to add on to the security features of Bitcoin wallets. They represent a form of storage known as cold storage – this is where the holder of Bitcoin does not wish to keep their money online or on any server therefore keeps it as 'its raw form of currency': either as the physical coin, paper or on a hardware device.

First is the paper wallet. This wallet serves as the cheapest method of storing Bitcoin. It comes with two QR codes on its surface enabling the use and receipt of the cryptocurrency. Furthermore, given that the Bitcoin keys – the private codes that enable transactions to be carried out – are stored on the paper rather than online, the wallet serves as a much safer method of storage as it is not prone to hacking as with other software-based wallets.

This being said, let us get to the most advanced of these wallets: the hardware wallet.

Hardware wallets are physical gadgets, similar to mobile phones, which are dedicated to Bitcoin. They serve as holders of the electronic keys of the cryptocurrency and are therefore used to facilitate payment.

Unlike other wallets, you actually have to pay a significant sum of money to acquire this wallet with some going as high as $240. This is especially so because of the fact that they are limited in supply – very limited supply versus higher demand causes prices to go up. However, with such a price, there must be value and this is what these wallets offer.

The main wallets in this category include Ledger Nano, SatoshiLabs Trezor and KeepKey with other advancements in this space having already been made such as Boinym's heartbeat sensing wallet which uses the rhythm of the heartbeat for security purposes.

Of all the above, hardware wallets (cold storage systems) are preferred as unlike other wallets, they are not prone to hacking and are therefore safe. For the case of Bitcoin and Monero, similar advice is offered.

Given the value of the cryptocurrency and the resources necessary to obtain them, it is prudent for the user to avoid loss of the same. Therefore, any system that provides higher security to the user is preferred in this case, making the hardware wallets preferable. However, if one cannot buy these wallets, they can generate their own paper wallets for either Bitcoin or Monero. Both of these wallets are tamper-proof and have higher security as they are not prone to hacking as is the case for online storages.

Before investing

Disclaimer: This book does not supersede any financial advice given by a financial analyst, rather serves merely as an information toolkit that improves the reader's knowledge of the two cryptocurrencies. Investing in cryptocurrencies is risky and you can lose some or all your money in the process.

Before investing, readers need to understand the asset they are investing in innately. First, they need to and must carry out due diligence before investing.

Due Diligence

Due diligence is a process whereby the investor goes thorough the statements, processes and premises of the entity they wish to invest in for the investor to validate that what has been reported by the company in their statements is actually true. This is a process which may take time, however, most of it has been made easy by the strict laws that require disclosures and periodic releases of information to the public. In case you are not investing in a public company, you may be required to actually visit the premises of the entity as you conduct your due diligence as most of their information is held privately.

The need for due diligence cannot be underscored further as it is the one measure meant to ensure that you are not conned off of your money by unscrupulous individuals.

Term and Tools of Trade

Second, the trader will need to define the term of their trades – short-term or long-term – and devise different methods of assessing their asset prices over that term.

To do this, tools such as technical tools[10] and fundamental tools[11] exist. These tools help one understand different facets of the asset's price as well as its drivers. It is also important to point out that in most cases, technical tools are used by short-term traders (such as day-traders) while fundamental analysis ends up being used by long-term traders – mainly because they forecast the time before they recoup their investment and this will generally take more than one year or a minimum of six months.

Data Analysis

Despite analysis tools playing a key role in investments, the data used in the analysis plays a more pivotal role. As per the phrase 'garbage in garbage out', if the data used for analysis is bad, everything about the entire process follows suit making any conclusions arrived at to be erroneous. Investors should take time and find the best data for use in their analysis as it drives the

---

[10] Technical analysis is based on one's analysis of asset price movement patterns whereby the trader expects that the price patterns will recur and they will capitalize on them. In order to do this, different technical tools have been developed such as the Moving Average Convergence Divergence (MACD), Bollinger Bands, Relative Strength Index (RSI) etc.

[11] Fundamental analysis is based on the analysis of the asset's revenue, cash flow and risk drivers. Here, the financial statements are analyzed with an incline towards understanding the strength of their books and how risky these books are after which forecasts are made and based on the output from these, investments too are made.

conclusions reached upon.

One trusted site that is sure to deliver high quality data on cryptocurrencies is Kaggle.

Kaggle, a site formed by developers, has been at the forefront of storing cryptocurrency data. The data, which has been made publicly available – and can be accessed on https://www.kaggle.com/jessevent/all-crypto-currencies/data – will be pivotal in ensuring that one easily carries out and completes their data analysis process.

Trading Strategies

Now that we have completed our analysis, it is important for the reader to understand how to trade. Trading in cryptocurrencies differs from most other trades in that the volatility[12] in this market is quite high.

This therefore makes trading in cryptocurrencies riskier – as a result of higher volatility. Investors have therefore tried to combat this risk by coming up with newer strategies. One such strategy is the dollar-cost averaging strategy.

This strategy entails the investor investing smaller fixed amounts in an investment over different time periods. This allows them to

---

[12] Volatility in finance refers to the changes experienced in the asset prices over a particular time. If the prices are seen to be changing very fast and over very high ranges, it is said that the asset's price is more volatile while if the price remains within certain low or expected boundaries, it is more volatile.

schedule their investments slowly over time with investors buying more when the prices of the asset are lower and more when they are higher. As a result, their average purchase price of the asset stands to be lower than it would have been if they invested the entire amount at the previous higher price.

In the case of cryptocurrencies, it would be advisable to buy Bitcoin or Monero at a lower price – given the volatility of the assets, this price may fall or rise quickly over a short period of time – and hold them over time as this price rises. If their average price is lower, the gains accrued to this investor would be quite high, making them smart investors in the long run.

Another important strategy is to ensure one understands the coin's market capitalization[13]. While many people focus on the price of the coin – with the hope of purchasing it at a very low price of below $1 and selling it at a high price so as to maximize on the gains – the cryptocurrency space requires an analysis of the market capitalization. Generally, the market capitalization is a better indicator as to how far upwards a coin's price can rise. Cryptocurrencies with high market capitalization allude to one thing: the fact that the market has invested significantly in them and is still demanding more of the coin means that they have a higher belief in the future of the coin. This means that it is more trusted thus making it more difficult for the coin to fall in future.

---

[13] Market capitalization is defined as the market value of an asset. Its value is derived by multiplying the price of the asset by the total volume of the asset traded in the market. In the case of cryptocurrencies, the total volume is the number of coins in circulation.

Cryptocurrencies

Once these coins are purchased, it will be important to diversify[14]. Diversification ensures that the investor will not lose their money in case of a collapse in the market therefore catering to the risk of correlation between risk factors in different industries. As with any asset, it is important for investors to put some of their money in Bitcoin or Monero while putting some other money in other assets which are uncorrelated or negatively correlated with cryptocurrencies – such as bonds or gold. Through this, even during a period of downturn in cryptocurrencies, the investor will have mitigated the effect of this downturn on their portfolio as it will be offset by the upturn in the uncorrelated or negatively correlated asset.

Finally, investor would benefit from learning that the best time to invest in a cryptocurrency is now. Given that the prices of assets eventually end up rising, investing early in these assets is a sure way of benefiting from this price increases. This is especially so for the cryptocurrency market as its market capitalization has been rising at a drastic rate – having risen from $5.1 billion in the beginning of 2015 to $473 billion in the beginning of 2018. Such benefits, in the long run, are expected to accrue investors who put their money within this space.

Eventually, all the strategies employed will be based on the same trading concept, buy low and sell high. As such, investors would be

---

[14] Diversification is a finance concept that speaks to an investor not 'putting all their eggs in one basket'. Rather, investors are advised to put different percentages of their investments in different assets so as to ensure that they do not lose all their money in case of a collapse in a given sector in the market.

prudent to read a lot more on different investment strategies – similar to the dollar-cost averaging strategy – so as to gain more solid grounding in the investment field.

Risk-Reward and Emotions

Once the above two are done and the investor is comfortable of the risk-reward trade-off they expect, they can invest their money. There are, however, still some things they need to be weary of or avoid.

Investors need to alleviate their emotions from their investments. Given that investment has a personal feel to it as it directly impacts the money we have, this becomes a difficult thing to do. However, if an investor pegs their emotions to their investments, they end up being biased and making irrational investment decisions in the process. Second it for investors to beware of pump and dump strategies where individuals come together and continuously buy an asset in order to hike its price before dumping the asset to the market.

This is the reason why due diligence and valuation are ever-so important to investors as they help them find out the intrinsic value of an asset thus ensure that they can spot such a market movement as it occurs.

Finally, given that any asset is affected by information from countries and other regulatory bodies – especially for cryptocurrencies which are new to the market thus prone to regulatory changes by countries across the globe – it is important to follow global news. This will inform most of the decisions the investor makes and give them an understanding – with time – of

Cryptocurrencies

how different news events will affect the movement in the prices of a cryptocurrency.

Having understood this, investors can now begin to look into different investment options and evaluate their feasibility.

Epilogue part 3

It is clear that they (cryptocurrencies) have brought to the world great solutions not only their form but also in how they operate. These currencies have brought with them a revolution to the modern economics age by both changing the dynamics of most economics concept as well as integrating currencies with technology. This presents a new age to users of money as well as its regulators as Central Banks are now being made more aware of this development and its role in the world.

These forms of currency have brought promise and hope to individuals worldwide; their promises embedded in words such as decentralization – the elimination of third parties such as banks from the transaction table –, low to zero transaction costs, high speed transactions and high security. Most people have only been made aware of the above strengths akin to the new technology.

Over time, the world edges closer to their acceptance as we look forward to a cryptocurrency filled and driven world.

Part 4: Ripple vs Bitcoin

The battle of the cryptocurrencies

- Do want to diversify your bitcoin investments in other cryptocurrencies?

- Do you want to invest (more) in ripple and / or bitcoin?

- Do you want to know where to start?

- Do you want of an overview of the exchanges?

- Do you want of an overview of the wallet-types and wallets to store your new investment?

- Do you want to make an educated decision and investment?

Start reading this part of the book now.

This section will help you make an well informed decision about whether you should invest (more) in bitcoin, ripple or whatever cryptocurrency for that matter.

Here you will learn:

- history of both cryptocurrencies

- the problems these cryptocurrencies were designed to solve

- if they meet those promises in reality (speed, ease of use, safety, security)

- a detailed description of the big exchanges were you can acquire bitcoin and ripple

- a profound explanation of the different type of wallets to store your new investments and safety guidelines

- AND an overview of the different investment strategies you can follow

Cryptocurrencies

Bitcoin vs. Ripple: An Introduction

You have probably heard of cryptocurrencies, Bitcoin, and Ripple. Every day you wonder what these things are and the impact they have on your life. Some have told you that you can become a millionaire if you really take it seriously. There are of course testimonies of Bitcoin millionaires all over the internet. Do these testimonies sound too good to be true?

As if that is not enough, there are theories that Bitcoin and Ripple are a new currency with the same functionality as your normal money. Can you really buy pizza or pay for your morning coffee with Bitcoin or Ripple? Moreover, Bitcoin and Ripple are just two of the coins. There are thousands more. Is there any place for all these coins? Is it worth it to know the differences between all the coins?

Cryptocurrencies rely on their underlying technology. What is the technology that gives these cryptocurrencies the attention that they have been getting? It does not matter whether you just heard of Bitcoin yesterday or last year, what you need is to the underlying technology and principles. Bitcoin or Ripple is not just ordinary money. It needs the right mental orientation to understand.

If the cryptocurrencies are a new form of money, then what are their differences with the current monetary system? It is difficult to trust transactions that are carried over the internet. The truth is that there are millions of scams on the internet. How can you be sure that Bitcoin, Ripple, and other similar currencies are not scams? How do you validate their legitimacy?

You are certainly interested in knowing how the coins are issued. Are there any central banks that determine how many coins must be released to the general public? Are cryptocurrencies regulated the same way that fiat money is? Is it safe? Is it secure? How anonymous is it?

Let's assume that you have given the cryptocurrencies the benefit of doubt and want to own them. Where do you get or buy them? This is the fundamental question that you should ask and get a straight and satisfactory answer. The question of money should never be left unanswered or half-answered.

There are of course promises made by the cryptocurrencies. These promises include very fast transactions. In the real world, we are used to cross-border payments that take up to 3 days. We now have Bitcoin that claims to process the same transaction in 10 minutes. If it is Ripple, they claim to process the same transaction in less than 3 minutes.

Ripple claims that cross-border payments cost people up to $1.6 trillion a year. The same currencies promise payment transactions that cost little to nothing. Is this feasible for them? What and how do they stand to gain from this?

The currencies are said to be decentralized and not owned or controlled by any central entity. This sounds great but is it safe and secure? Are they any better than banks? When banks started off, they gave us incentives for banking with them. When we were hooked with them and relied on them, they turned on us and charged us. Are cryptocurrencies not going to turn on us in the future?

The truth is that there is a lot to learn and know. This book will give you all the information you need to know about Bitcoin and Ripple.

Cryptocurrencies

It will touch on their fundamental differences. It will also touch on their similarities such as decentralization, anonymity, near-zero transaction fees, speed, and security. This book answers all those questions and more.

Bitcoin

Bitcoin is very famous. I would not expect any less from Bitcoin especially considering its paradigm shift in allowing secure transactions on its network. There are a few who really have no idea what Bitcoin is. There are, however, a few people who truly understand what Bitcoin is and what it can do. The point here is that there is a major difference between being aware of Bitcoin and knowing what it is. The aim of this chapter is to take elevate your awareness to knowledge. Knowledge is power. Our forefathers have held this mantra in high regards and I am sure we can do the same without any harm.

Our first stop is to look at the history of Bitcoin. The history of Bitcoin is pretty fascinating because there are pre-Bitcoin and post-Bitcoin history. The pre-Bitcoin history touches on the series of events that occurred before Bitcoin was described and presented to the world. You could call this the warm-up if this was a football match.

Secondly, I am going to touch a bit about post-Bitcoin history. I am referring to the series of events that happened after the invention of Bitcoin. Bitcoin was not just invented and everything stopped there. Things changed. Another gold rush emerged. You have probably heard of the "Scramble for Africa" a few centuries ago. Something similar happened when people knew about Bitcoin. Bitcoin changed many things. If redefined what we thought we knew about our monetary system. Importantly, it has laid down the foundation for something far more reaching.

Pre-history of Bitcoin

In my own opinion, the pre-history of Bitcoin starts with the creation of the fiat monetary system and the moment computers were introduced to the world. Each revolution or new era is mainly pioneered by the flaws in the previous system. There may be no flaws sometimes but there is a need to upgrade to a new and better system.

Before the current monetary system of coins and paper notes was introduced, people exchanged goods and services through barter trading. This was a system flawed with so many inconsistencies and unfairness. There was no standard unit upon which goods/services could be measured. It simply thrived on surplus and demand.

It was many years before there was an ingenious idea to invent coins and paper money. A new standard was defined. The current fiat money system was born and it proved to be more efficient than barter trade. Mind you, barter trade still exists today. A few centuries and a couple of decades later, computers were introduced to the world. At the same time, the principle of countries and borders had already been established an in full force. Each country had its own currency whose strength depended on a number of factors. People from different countries could exchange goods and services. Banks were already in place and they could handle such transactions.

On the other hand, the people who were pioneering digital technology were now pushing for digital cash. They wanted to build a digital currency that matched the digital times they were living in. A lot of varied platforms and digital cash protocols were built by many digital experts of the time. David Chaum notably pioneered the ecash protocol, Nick Szabo worked on bit gold while Wei Dai introduced something known as b-money. All these were efforts to find a true digital currency that would replace the fiat monetary system or at least, exist alongside it. These projects were not failures because they laid down the groundwork for what was to come. This is probably a very important period because it is the one that inspired the idea of a digital currency system. However, the technology necessary to build such a cash system was still lacking.

Then in 2008, when hope was faded but not yet completely gone, the internet welcomed a new domain, "bitcoin.org." This was just a simple domain that was to change many things. A few weeks later, the white paper entitled *Bitcoin: A Peer-to-Peer Electronic Cash System* was presented to cryptography experts and enthusiasts. A new currency was being invented in the shadows. This famous white paper was written by an unknown person/programmer by the name Satoshi Nakamoto. The true identity of Satoshi Nakamoto is a big debate that requires a book of its own.

When the Bitcoin network was implemented in 2009, its first users were Hal Finney, Nick Szabo, and Wei Dai. This comes as no surprise as they were the same people who pioneered the groundwork for digital cash long before Bitcoin was conceived. The original creator of Bitcoin, Satoshi, mined close to a million coins of his currency before vanishing into thin air. Gavin Andresen ran the show when the Satoshi bailed out. We don't know if this was a bailout or a strategic exit meant to shield him/her from the public face.

The value of Bitcoin was close to nothing then. People negotiated what they thought was the true value of the coin. There is even a story that a programmer paid for 2 pizzas with 10,000 BTC. Bitcoin had not yet gone mainstream then and I guess the programmer thought he had hit a jackpot. However, slowly, Bitcoin began to grab the attention of many people. To start off, Bitcoin mainly appealed to programmers due to the complex nature of the technology behind it. It is not something that your average Tom, Dick, and Harry would easily understand on any given sunny or rainy day.

2011 was a busy year for Bitcoin. The first fork took place and a new currency was formed. The new currency was called Litecoin. It was spearheaded by Charlie, an ex-employee of Google. Litecoin and a host of other coins that were created that year were known as Altcoins. There were called that because they were simply alternatives to the Bitcoin. Online organizations like WikiLeaks accepted Bitcoins. Bitcoin was now functioning as a currency.

From 2012, many organizations, governments, and government departments took notice of Bitcoin. Bitcoin exchanges were banned in Thailand in 2013. There was a surge in the people who were making transactions using Bitcoin. Bitcoin was becoming more popular and resulted in the creation of several other competing currencies or coins. China's central bank banned the use of Bitcoins. Bitcoin and other cryptocurrencies have had a torrid time in Asian countries with China and Korea being the main culprits. Bitcoin machines were being installed in their thousands in the United States signaling the unofficial acceptance of the digital currency as a medium of exchange.

On the exchanges, the price of Bitcoin was volatile and

unpredictable. It would go up and down just like that. One notable thing about Bitcoin is its ability to pick up its price after any major or minor slide. Many people called it a bubble and predicted that it would burst, but each time, it has managed to disappoint them.

Blockchain technology: the main driver behind the success of Bitcoin and cryptocurrencies

Bitcoin is a project that was in the making for many years. Although there isn't much information on the creator of Bitcoin, I can tell you that Bitcoin's success lies partly in blockchain technology. The early attempts to create a digital cash were unsuccessful due to lack of technology that supported the idea. The blockchain is the technology that they were looking for. The word blockchain has been thrown around many times. You hear people talk about it at parties, or over a braai and tech ladies probably talk about at bridal showers. You do not need to feel out of place simply because no one has given you a simple-to-understand yet convincing explanation of the blockchain is.

A blockchain is a distributed public ledger that is used to store and record valuable data and information. The blockchain is governed by the following set of rules:

- Immutable – information entered on the blockchain database cannot be erased or altered.

- Decentralized – this is one of the most attractive attributes of blockchain technology. It is decentralized in the sense that there is no single location where transactions are stored on the network. The transactions exist on every computer on the network. Imagine a situation where we wake to the news that Google servers have been burnt down. The new would be catastrophic but it does not mean the end of the world. You can still search for information on other search engines such as Yahoo and Bing. The internet is not centralized and has no single point of failure. This is how a blockchain network is designed. The only way to take down a blockchain network is to corrupt or destroy all the computers on the network. Trust me, this is not an easy task.

- Transparency – the blockchain network is very transparent due to the fact that every transaction is verified by every computer on the network. The transaction can only be processed if it has been verified by all the members of the network.

- Cryptographically secure – the blockchain network uses the advanced method of cryptography to secure its transactions. This makes the network more secure and less susceptible to attacks and hacks.

- Anonymity – the transactions on the blockchain network are anonymous. Although network users are required to verify each transaction, they have no way of knowing who is making the transaction.

Uses and theories of Bitcoin

Bitcoin is a currency that can be used the same way as the US$ or the Euro. However, it is a currency with a difference. I have talked about its history and revolutionary groundbreaking technology. What I haven't really done is tell you what Bitcoin is and how it works.

Bitcoin is a cryptocurrency that belongs to alternative, digital, and virtual currencies. It is a currency that is generated by computer software and in essence, it may just be a string of zeros and ones.

This is because this is how everything in the digital world is presented as. It is alternative in the sense that it an alternative to the current fiat monetary system. Finally, we come to the part that I like most. There is nothing really special about this part. I just enjoy explaining it to people.

It is a virtual currency because this it does not exist in the physical world that same way your paper money and coins exist. No one has ever seen or touched a Bitcoin. Never mind the images you on the internet with a big B. That's not a Bitcoin. Technically speaking, no one owns a Bitcoin. What you simply own is an address to the location of your virtual money. That address has a record of how much currency you have. What you own is a set of private and public keys. The private key is similar to the key to your home or apartment. It's what give you access to your digital currency. It is only known to you. Whoever gets access to your private key has access to your Bitcoins. In the real world, banks and people have safes to keep their money far from prying eyes. You cannot build a safe for your Bitcoins. You can only build a safe for your private keys. Think of your Bitcoins as the money in your bank and the credit card pin number as your private key. Whoever has access to your credit card and pin number also has access to the money in your bank.

The public key is like your bank account. Although you need to keep it safe, it does not matter if it gets in the public eye. In fact, you want it to be in the public eye. The public key is the address to your money. People can only send you Bitcoins through the public key. This is the same way that people send you money using your bank account number.

Cryptocurrencies

You can use Bitcoins to make purchases or settle debts. However, the principles are quite different from what you are used to. Let's assume you want to send your child some money or pay for your morning muffins at a local café. This is all that happens.

- A request is lodged with you.

- The request is openly broadcast on the transparent Peer-to-Peer network of computers. Each computer on the P2P network is known as a node.

- The transactions are validated by the network nodes

- The verified and validated transaction is grouped together with other similar transactions. This creates a new data block.

- The newly created block becomes part of the network and this completes the transaction.

Bitcoin transactions

Bitcoin was in a way introduced so that it could address some of the challenges that the banking infrastructure was failing to deliver to the population in the modern times. It is a known fact that sometimes transactions can take as long as 3 -5 business days to clear. This is a long wait especially if you want to use the money for something urgent. Secondly, the transactions are very costly and result in people losing a large chunk of their money. This is one way that banks are profiteering from. Bitcoin aims to correct this in several ways.

- No third-party involved – when you want to send some money to someone, you rely on a bank or other intermediary party to do so. The third-party requires a fee to do this. With Bitcoin, you can send your money to your desired person without worrying about a third party.

- Transaction costs – I just mentioned the cost you pay to an intermediary party who facilitates the transactions. The Bitcoin eliminates the need for a third party with significantly minimizes the money you pay. More importantly, you should be glad to hear to hear that Bitcoin charges near-zero for all the transactions on its network.

- Security – the Bitcoin network is secure due to decentralization. There is no central point that hackers can target before taking down the network. --

- Anonymous – the transactions are anonymous and no one will ever know when you make a transaction. The nodes on the Bitcoin network can only verify the transaction.

- Transaction speed – while banks may take up to 3 days to process a transaction, the same transaction is completed within 10 minutes on the Bitcoin network.

Ripple

Ripple is one of the popular Altcoins. It is one of the top five cryptocurrencies by market capitalization. Apart from being one of the digital assets that have caused a stir in the financial and investment world, what else can be said about Ripple? There is a lot to talk and write about. My first port of call would be its interesting history. Yes, the history is interesting in the sense that the foundations of Ripple go long back before Bitcoin came into the picture. If you want, you can call it a currency or network that survived in two separate timelines.

The early roots of Ripple are found in Vancouver, Canada. A developer by the name of Ryan Fugger quietly worked on developing the decentralized monetary system. This system, known as Ripplepay, made it possible for people to construct their own currencies. It was not too different from cryptocurrencies that were yet to come. Jed McCaleb was inspired by this system and eventually created the eDonkey network. He was helped by Arthur Britto and David Schwartz to build the network. Probably inspired by Bitcoin and some of its underpinning technologies, the trio started working on building a digital currency protocol similar to Bitcoin. However, it deviated a bit from Bitcoin in that there was no mining involved. This resulted in a huge cut in electricity usage. Secondly, the new system had faster transaction speed compared to Bitcoin. All this work was done in 2011.

The team brought in Chris Larsen in August 2012. Larsen was no stranger in creating online businesses as he had formerly founded E-Loan and Prosper. McCaleb and Larsen held talks with Fugger which resulted in the pair assuming control of Ripplepay. In

September of the same year, OpenCoin Inc. was founded. OpenCoin went on to design a new payment system know the Ripple Transaction Protocol. The system borrowed several of its ideas from Fugger's Ripplepay project. The new protocol was very revolutionary and allowed any two parties to send each other money without the need of an intermediary. This marginally reduced the transaction fees and processing time. To add icing on the cake, OpenCoin was backed by several prominent investors such as Google Ventures and Andreessen Horowitz.

McCaleb eventually left Ripple and founded Stellar, a director competitor of Ripple. It is alleged that he left amid disagreements with Larsen. These are only allegations. McCaleb went on to announce that he would be selling all the XRP tokens he owned. That resulted in lawsuits that stopped McCaleb from selling all his tokens at once. It is believed that such an act would have hurt Ripple.

Ripple at a glance

If you have heard of Bitcoin or know what it is, then you have an idea of what Ripple is. Ripple is something similar to Bitcoin but with a different underlying functionality. Ripple may also be confusing because of its dual role. Ripple can refer to a payment protocol or Ripple network's native currency known as the Ripple token (XRP). If you truly want to know what Ripple is, you have to start by make a clear distinction between the two.

The Ripple protocol is an open source global payment network that facilitates global payments at near zero cost and near-instantaneous speed. Ripple is simply in the remittance business. Think of Ripple as the modern Western Union updated with several upgrades. Ripple Company argues that the global payment infrastructure was designed when discos were still the best thing that ever happened to the world. Some of you may not even know what a disco is. There are major flaws in the current payment structure and this is what Ripple intends to address.

To begin with, global transactions take between 3 – 5 days to go through. This is a lot of time by any standards. You have probably heard that "times is money." If this is true, then you can't afford to wait for almost a week before a transaction goes through. Secondly, the cost for such transactions is enormously high. It is estimated by Ripple that people are losing more than $1.6 trillion in annual transaction fees. This is a lot of money that people could keep in their pockets if there is a new system that addresses this issue with the merit it deserves.

You know that "change is the only constant thing in the world." It is high time that there is a change in the payment system. Ripple is that change that people want. Lastly, the current payment system is unreliable and unacceptable.

The Ripple Protocol

The protocol may certainly be a game changer in the global payments sector. The Ripple payment protocol allows you to send and receive any asset of value. This can be gold, fiat money, etc. The Ripple protocol was designed to be adopted by banks to aid them in their global transactions. It has so far been adopted by several banks and financial firms such as American Express.

The actual process that enables Ripple to send money globally is a bit complex. However, I will try to simplify it as much as possible without oversimplifying it. You can understand how Ripple works if we start off with practical examples. Let us say you are in Japan and want to send your friend in Nigeria some money. What normally happens is that the Japanese Yen you deposit into a bank are converted into one of the mainstream currencies such the US$. This conversion incurs conversion expenses. The dollars are sent to the bank in Nigeria. However, the bank in Nigeria can only issue the money in Naira (native currency used in Nigeria) to your friend and not in dollars. The conversion process from US$ to Naira costs some money. You also have to pay the cost of the transaction fee. Moreover, this process takes days to process. In summary, this is a multi-step process that takes time and costs a substantial amount of money.

If you are going to do the same transaction on the Ripple network, you will be doing yourself a big favor. The Ripple protocol looks for the easiest and quickest route to use for such a transaction. The overall goal is to have a near-instantaneous transaction that costs you almost nothing. Ripple simply bypasses some of the steps that you would go through if your use intermediaries for your global transaction.

Let's now go on and try to understand what goes on under the hood of Ripple. I am referring to the actual technology behind technology. The Ripple protocol a Peer-to-peer public ledger system controlled by validating nodes. Transactions on the network are processed by these nodes. A transaction is sent to the Ripple network before it is processed. It is at this point that the Ripple sequence starts. The process is as follows:

- The creation of a new transaction

Cryptocurrencies

- The transaction is publicized on the network by all the individual servers. The Ripple server software runs on a server.

- Transactions from all the servers are pooled together so that voting can occur.

- Each transaction must receive a set number of votes before it can proceed to the next round of the process. Transactions that do not receive the minimum number of votes discarded or sent back in line for voting.

- Each transaction needs a minimum of 80% votes. A transaction that achieves this minimum or more becomes part of the ledger.

- The process ends when the transaction gets added to the ledger system.

Difference between Bitcoin and other Altcoins

It is common knowledge that Ripple is a new digital asset that is classified in the same that Bitcoin is classified. Ripple is not very similar to Bitcoin. In fact, there a quite a number of differences between the two. Some of these differences are important in shaping the success of Ripple as a payment protocol and digital currency. Some of the notable differences are outlined below.

- Transaction speed – compared to Bitcoin and other Altcoins, Ripple processes transactions at the speed of light. Transactions that take up to 4 days via conventional banks can take up to 10 minutes on the Bitcoin network to be validated. The same transaction takes only 5 – 10 seconds on the Ripple network. This is insanely fast.

- Method of currency issue – you know that the money in your country is issued and controlled by your central bank. If Bitcoin and Ripple XRP token are a currency, then there should be a way by which they are issued. Bitcoin is obtained by a process known as mining. Mining is an activity that involves solving complex mathematical equations. The miners are rewarded with Bitcoins. The computers used to carry the mining process are very powerful and require a lot of electrical energy.

- Ripple is pre-mined. This basically means that Ripple tokens do not need to be mined the same way that Bitcoins are mined. This saves electrical energy a lot.

- Cheaper costs – the Ripple protocol charges a small fee for carrying out transactions on the network. This fee does not go into anyone's pocket but is rather destroyed. The purpose of the network is to prevent a single entity from 'clogging' the network if the transactions were free. The fee is used as an anti-spam measure.

Cryptocurrencies

- The cap on the currency – Bitcoin was designed in such a way that there will ever be 21 million coins in existence. This makes the currency scarce at some point and mining activities will cease to exist. However, Ripple uses a different approach. The Ripple tokens are destroyed after every transaction and this has a few consequences. The supply of Ripple tokens will start to deflate at some point. The currency will become scarce. There is a major difference between Bitcoin's constant supply of 21 million coins and Ripple's deflating currency.

- Relationship with banks – while Bitcoin and the majority of Altcoins were built to directly compete with banks, the Ripple protocol was built to work with banks. This is where Ripple totally deviates from other digital currencies.

- Decentralization – cryptocurrencies are based on blockchain technology. Blockchain technology allows the digital assets to be decentralized. Decentralization does not support having a central point of authority. The Ripple protocol is not fully decentralized but is making plans to be fully decentralized in the future.

There are major differences between Bitcoin and Ripple. However, they are all grouped as digital assets. Surprisingly though, Ripple is older than Bitcoin, the firstborn of all cryptocurrencies. Just imagine being older than your elder brother/sister. That makes you Ripple.

Real world examples

Cryptocurrencies have in a way, brought some kind of confusion into the world. But this is the good kind of confusion. It is easy for you to earn a slap on your cheek if you tell someone that Bitcoin is a currency. How can Bitcoin be money? What qualifies it to be treated with the same respect as the US$ or the British Pound. It may be easier to explain this to a younger generation but explaining that to your old grandmother is nothing more than a suicide mission.

However, before I validate that Bitcoin is currency or why it should be treated as such, let's take a trip down a memory lane. A long trip down the memory lane. I will take you on a journey about the history of money. I will look at where we started and how we arrived where we are today. You must always remember that the world has always been controlled by change and evolution.

Money has shown us that it obeys that fundamental trend of the world. The evolution of money is not one that is characterized by greed or ulterior motives, but nature's forces of change. The history of money dates as back as the birth of the world. A long time ago, when the world was still primitive, people had to find a way to trade. Mathematics had not yet been developed and the number system as we know it was not yet developed. Even in those archaic and undesirable conditions, people still needed to find a way to trade.

They found such a way through barter trade. Barter trade is a system in which trade is facilitated by literary exchanging goods. The method obviously had its flaws especially given that there were no standards to govern how exchanges were made. To some extent, the system also relied on supply and demand. If I had excess grain but little fabric, I will go and exchange my grain for fabric. I think problems arose on deciding how much grain was worth a certain amount of fabric.

With time, men became a bit more adventurous and discovered minerals and precious metals. Gold was found to be the most precious of them all. High value was placed on it. It immediately became the new standard method of trade. It surpassed barter trade. Gold became the first currency in the world.

For so many years, gold remained the standard and measure of one's wealth. In the 13th century, the Chinese people invented coins. This was the humble beginning of what we call money today. This new invention had several advantages that led to its gradual and mass adoption. That was the beginning of a new era in the financial world.

Banks came into existence and people had the opportunity to save their money. They even earned an interest on their investments. This was an exciting moment. Money could be sent from one bank to another. Innovation had arrived. People from different countries could conduct businesses with each other with the trust that banks would handle the payment part. And banks did a god job.

But monochromatic televisions were still great. There was no Facebook then. The idea of a smartphone was just a genius' dream. The infrastructure for intercontinental financial transactions was put in place then. Technology and innovation were taking great strides in the right direction. Even in the light of this innovation and accelerated growth, there were still a lot of shortcomings.

The transactions were getting processed at a snail's pace. Transactions took days to be transferred from one country to the next. The prices were for the bank transactions were very high. But nobody complained. It was the choice that people had at the time.

Some of the most visionary people at the time were already working on a new project to invent digital cash. The digital cash would serve the same purpose as fiat money but with some modifications. It was obviously supposed to address the issues of safety, transaction speed, and many more. Many people worked on new ways to create a digital cash. It would be unfair to call these endeavors as complete failures. These are the projects that laid down the foundation for cryptocurrencies.

In 2009, the financial foundations were shaken. Bitcoin was invented. It was introduced to the world. Change and innovation had arrived. Bitcoin lead to the creation of many other Altcoins including Ripple.

The earlier chapters have touched a bit about Bitcoin and Ripple. I will not go over them. However, I will shed more light on a few more issues.

The safety of Bitcoin and Ripple

The safety of Bitcoin and Ripple. It stems from two fundamental questions. Each of the questions carries a lot of weight and needs to be addressed before anyone decides to own any of the cryptocurrencies. The first question is the longtime safety of owning cryptocurrencies. Will Bitcoin and Ripple still be viable in the next coming few years or they will be worth nothing? Secondly, how secure is it to store cryptocurrencies given that the transactions have to be approved by millions of computers on the network? I will address these very important questions methodically.

How can you be guaranteed about the future value of Bitcoin? The short and straight answer is that you cannot. But how did someone who invested in Bitcoin in 2009 or 2010 knew that Bitcoin would be worth almost $20,000 in December 2017? The person didn't know that or even dream of it. But they still went on to invest in it. This is the situation you find yourself in. Should you buy Bitcoins or Ripple? Let's go all over it slowly without including the overwhelming figures.

Bitcoin and Ripple are new currency powered by technology and value. As long as they both continue to serve a purpose and are supported by efficient and relevant technologies, they may live long enough to see the next millennia. I can tell you that Bitcoin and Ripple have changed the way that financial transactions are carried out. And this is only just the beginning. The first half of Bitcoin's nine-year existence has generally been about acceptance and being known to all the people in the world. It was quite difficult at first but it finally has the attention of the world.

It may not be a mainstream currency at the moment but it has made itself known. It has also opened the doors for other cryptocurrencies that are backed by real technology such Ripple. Secondly, Bitcoin has gathered the attention of authorities, regulators, and lawmakers. It has graduated from being the pass time project of computer geniuses to be a topic worth discussing at some of the world's most prestigious events. Think of events like the World Economic Forum. In a way, it is a sign that Bitcoin and Altcoins may become mainstream in the next coming years.

The majority may have heard of the crackdown on Bitcoin exchanges in Asian countries. China was at the forefront of this operation followed by South Korea. Does this spell the doom of Bitcoin and Altcoins? Contrary to the popular belief, this is just the beginning. It shows that Bitcoin is strong enough to gain the attention of authorities. At some point, there has to be regulation on how cryptocurrencies operate in this world. Just keep in mind that they are challenging the territories that have previously belonged to powerful organizations and institutions that have controlled the world for a very long time.

Do I think that Bitcoin will be dumped in the next few years? No. I think that its mass adoption is simply on course. It may not be the mainstream currency in the next few years but its grip on the financial system will increase. It is an investment worth a lot in the future.

The second and equally important question is the safety of owning Bitcoin. Where do you keep them and how do ensure their security? Do you need a safe deposit box for them? Yes, you may need a safe deposit box if you decide to store your Bitcoins in a hardware wallet. How strong is the Bitcoin or Ripple network and how easily can it be attacked? This is where blockchain technology gets interesting?

The safety of Bitcoin depends on the blockchain network. The Bitcoin network is an enormous network of computers running Bitcoin software. Each transaction is controlled and monitored by

Cryptocurrencies

these computers which are owned by people known as miners. Miners can be added and removed from the network without affecting the network. Each transaction that you carry out on the Bitcoin network is first checked by all the computers on the network. The transaction is validated so as to ensure that there is transparency. Does this make the network impenetrable? No, not at all. The network can be breached and hostage.

This is only true theoretically. In practice, it is a big challenge that will give hackers a good run for its money and computing power. A hacker would have to redo all the work that all the miners on the Bitcoin network do. This requires a lot of power that may not even be compensated by the successful hack. In this regard, it is almost impossible and unthinkable for someone to try and hack the Bitcoin network.

However, there is "A 51% Attack" theory. Mining is now being done by mining pools. A mining pool is a group of miners that work together as a single unit by uniting all their computing power. If a mining pool or single entity can manage to control 51% network, then it can potentially disrupt the entire network. The entity suspends ongoing and legitimate transactions resulting in double spend. Think of double spend as counterfeit money.

The truth is that Bitcoin is a very strong but like any other system, it can be exploited. However, it will be a long time before that happens. In the past, there have been several heists of Bitcoins worth millions. It is important to note that the heists were not as a result of Bitcoin network's weakness but as a result of vulnerabilities found in the wallets storing Bitcoins.

One more thing that you may be wondering about is the anonymity of Bitcoin. Bitcoin is not entirely anonymous. It has been believed to be anonymous because of a number of reasons. These are some of the reasons why Bitcoin has been thought to be anonymous.

Bitcoin addresses are important in carrying out transactions on the network. Unlike bank accounts that are tied to a person's identity, Bitcoin addresses do not require you to produce your personal details.

Bitcoin transactions are not depended on the identity of the people who use the network. They are tied to private and public keys. You can send Bitcoins to someone without them needing to know who you are.

However, it is theoretically possible for the identity of Bitcoin users to be discovered. A person/hacker/official can connect several computers to the Bitcoin network and collate the data to pinpoint where transactions came from. This requires a lot of work but it can be done.

Mining

While the central bank in your country issues and controls the distribution of money, Bitcoins are issued and distributed differently. There is no one entity responsible for the currency issue but rather uses a process known as mining. Mining is done by miners and these people are at the core of the Bitcoin network.

Miners serve two purposes. They solve complex mathematical puzzles with the hope of winning a Bitcoin as the grand prize. Secondly, they validate transactions on the Bitcoin network. Mining is not a simple process but a very complex and energy-intensive process. Miners use energy-hungry to do their job and this comes with a hefty electrical bill.

Some analysts argue that mining is a digital process that turns electrical energy into money.

You may wonder and argue if mining in necessary in the Bitcoin ecosystem. Mining is absolutely necessary because it is the only way of ensuring that new coins are created and distributed on the network. The mining can be done by anyone who has the computing power to do so. This means that there is no central system controlling Bitcoins.

As more and more people chose the mining path, the complexity of the puzzles to be solved has increased. This is to control the number of Bitcoins in circulation. If more people can mine it, the supply might surpass the demand and the value of Bitcoin will decrease. Bitcoin mining is very important. It provides some degree of control in the ecosystem.

The biggest drawback is the high energy consumption which may be contributing to climate change. As of December 2017, it was estimated Bitcoin mining activities require about 31 Terawatt Hours annually. As a result, Bitcoin mining activities use more energy than that used by 159 small individual countries. It is estimated that Bitcoin mining uses more electrical energy than the U.S. in 2019. It is further estimated that Bitcoin mining will match the world's entire energy requirements in 2020. This is where many people believe that Bitcoin is inefficient.

On the other hand, Ripple is not mined but pre-mined. This means that all the Ripple tokens were created before the network was launched. The Ripple creators only release a certain amount of tokens to the public at regular intervals. There are no energy requirements here. Unfortunately, this method defeats the purpose of a decentralized currency.

This means that Ripple tokens are controlled by a few people. These people can crash the market if they want to through pump and dump. The purpose of cryptocurrencies was to decentralize their control so that on one particular person or group of people could have a firm grip on the control of a currency.

However, from an energy point of view, Ripple has better functionality.

Cryptocurrencies

How to buy Bitcoin and Ripple

Buying Bitcoin, Ripple or any other cryptocurrency is not a walk in the park. It is very different from going to the grocery store and buying your favorite items. However, with some knowledge, you can find that buying cryptocurrencies is not that much of a mountain to climb. I will start by saying that you need a digital wallet before buying cryptocurrencies. I will come to that in the next topic chapter.

The best way to buy cryptocurrencies is to use exchanges. I will give you a complete list of exchanges that you can use. There are a few things that you need to be on the look-out for before you choose your preferred exchange.

- Cost and fees – most exchanges will charge for using their services. You need to be aware of these fees before making your first transaction. You don't want to cry foul afterward

- Payment set-up – be sure to check how people are allowed to buy cryptocurrencies. The methods used can be PayPal, bank transfer or debit & credit card. Look for an exchange that accommodated your preferred and convenient method of payment.

- Verification process – some of the major Bitcoin exchanges requires you to verify your identity. Identity verification is important because it protects you from criminal activities. It also allows you to operate in a safe environment.

- Reputation and reviews – take your time to read the reviews of an exchange before signing up. A good website will have positive reviews.

- Compare exchange rates – the exchanges do not operate at the same rate. Look for one with favorable rates.

- Geographic restrictions – the majority of the exchanges limit their services to certain regions and countries. Check to see if your favorite exchange provides its services to people in your region or area.

An exchange is a platform for converting cryptocurrencies or fiat money. Exchanges work differently but the following is common to all of them:

- Have a legal account – open an account with the exchange of your choice. You may be required to verify your identity.

- Deposit fiat or crypto – you will need to buy cryptocurrencies using fiat money or cryptocurrencies. If you want to buy cryptocurrencies for the first time, it is better to settle for exchanges that accept fiat money.

- Withdrawal – you can send your cryptocurrencies to a new and safe crypto address.

- There are, as expected, some differences between the hundreds of exchanges out there. You must take note of the differences as they are very important. Your job is to seek an exchange that is aligned with your short-term and long-term goals.

- Coins supported – exchanges don't support the same coins. Others only specialize in Bitcoins while others the major coins such as Ethereum, Ripple, and Litecoin. Be sure of the coins that you want to buy first and check if the exchanges have support for your coins.

- Fiat support – go for exchanges that support payment through credit/debit cards or bank transfers.

- Fees charged – this is particularly important. You do not want to lose your money over some high charges. Exchanges can either charge you for trading through their platform or making withdrawals and deposits.

Exchange types – there are three types of exchanges.

- Broker – brokers buy cryptocurrencies from exchanges and sell them on their own and usually higher price. They will obviously be expensive to buy from but the process is simple.

- Trading platforms – this is a trading platform with advanced algorithms to trade cryptocurrency pairs.

- P2P marketplace – a P2P marketplace is interesting in the way it functions. It matches buyers and sellers together. It does not process any transaction.

I have compiled a short list of some of the popular exchanges that you can use to buy and sell your cryptocurrencies.

Coinbase

Coinbase was established in 2011 by Fred Ehrsam and Brian Armstrong. The exchange began offering its services in 2012. It is estimated that the California-based exchange has more than 13.3 million users of November 2017. It accepts fiat currencies from 32 countries and provides its services to residents of more than 190 countries globally. The exchange deals with Bitcoin, Ether, Bitcoin Cash, and Litecoin.

Coinbase allows you to buy cryptocurrencies with a debit or credit card and bank transfers. Coinbase requires you to do a full identification verification. This includes uploading your ID document as well as latest proof of residence.

The exchange has limits on the amount you transact per day. A verified U.S. person can transact Bitcoins worth $50,000 per day. European customers are required to have a maximum balance of €30,000 in their Coinbase account. Coinbase allows you to create a wallet that you can use to keep your wallet. As a side rule, store your digital wealth far away from exchanges.

Coinmama

Coinmama is an Israeli-based Bitcoin exchange. It is famous for accepting payments through credit and debit cards. However, it charges a high fee of 6%. It serves a large number of countries except for a few that are under sanctions.

It has been in the industry for quite a long time. You can make transactions worth $150 or less (in Bitcoins) without verifying your ID. You need to an ID verification if you want to make bigger transactions. The exchange enables you to make daily purchases that are not worth more than $5,000 in Bitcoins. Your monthly limit is $20,000.

Poloniex

Poloniex was established in 2014 by Tristan D'Agosta. The exchange was hacked in the same year and lost 12.3% of customer Bitcoins. Ever since then, the company has tirelessly to improve its security. It currently stores all cryptocurrencies in cold storage. It only keeps enough cryptocurrencies to facilitate daily trading. The exchange has an auditing program that constantly monitors the platform. The aim is to pick any strange activities before they cause a major problem. The platform's 2-Factor Authentication is a good security feature.

The exchange allows you to buy, send, and trade over 100 currencies including Bitcoin and Ripple. Coinmama charges depending on the Bitcoin amount being transacted. Transactions can take as long as 30 minutes to 1 hour to be completed.

The withdrawal limit on the platform is based on verification. Unverified account holders can only withdraw up to $2,000. Verification increases the limit amount to $25,000. The verification process requires your ID, proof of address and sometimes, your selfie holding your ID credentials.

There is a higher level of verification that can allow withdrawing more than $25,000. The best place to find this information is to contact the platform's support center.

Kraken

Kraken was founded in 2011 in San-Francisco. The exchange allows trading in Euro, US dollar, Canadian dollar, Japanese yen, and the British pound. Kraken has managed to expand over the years due to its ability to its acquisition of companies such as CryptoWatch.

Kraken is a notable exchange because it is trusted by the Japanese government and has the blessing of European banks.

The platform is conducive for professional traders due to its liquidity, rich features, and its speed. It is very secure and transparent. It allows you to buy a variety of currencies including Bitcoin, Ripple, Ether, Litecoin, Bitcoin Cash, Ether Classic, EOS, etc.

The exchange does not allow payments through PayPal and debit and credit cards. However, wire transfers are allowed. Wire transfers are processed within 1 – 5 business days. Kraken is known for its low transaction fees.

Kraken requires you to verify your identity before you can start buying cryptocurrencies. You will have to provide your ID document and proof of residence.

Blockchain.info

Blockchain.info wallet is an online wallet that you can use using any browser of your choice. It also has a mobile version that you can use. The online version has a 2-Factor-Authentication (2FA) which makes it more secure.

The blockchain is a popular wallet and can be used to store Bitcoin and Ethereum. It has an easy-to-use wallet. It has an informative bar at the bottom that allows users to see the number of daily transactions. Some of its major selling points include:

- Blockchain.info is one of the most well-known companies in the crypto industry
- Suited for small regular payments
- Easy to use
- The smartphone makes the wallet more interesting to use

How to store

In the real world, you store your fiat money in bank accounts, safes, pockets, or wallets. Cryptocurrencies are stored slightly differently. They are stored in digital wallets. I will go over the definition of a digital currency before telling you what a digital wallet.

A cryptocurrency is a virtual currency that you can neither touch nor feel. It is simply a record of transactions. You don't really own the currency. What you simply own is the public and private keys. The public key is the address you give people to send you money while the private key allows you access to your money.

A digital wallet is simply a software program or hardware that allows you to generate public and private keys. It receives your digital cash and allows you to spend it. There are two types of storage. Hot and cold. Hot storage refers to any wallet that stores your private keys online. This is a bit dangerous as it exposes your wealth to hackers and attackers. Cold storage means the opposite. It is any digital wallet that is not connected to the internet.

There are several types of wallets. Let's go over them.

Desktop wallet

This is a wallet program installed on your desktop or laptop. You can only access on the machine that it was installed on. You can only lose your money if you lose your gadget. Fortunately, the majority of desktop wallets now come with backup plans. A desktop wallet is a secure option.

Exodus is a good example of a desktop wallet. Although considered to be an online wallet, the Exodus wallet supports several coins including Bitcoin, Ethereum, EOS, etc. The wallet also supports several fiat currencies including the US dollar, Japanese Yen, etc.

The wallet allows you to back up your data which is a good security measure. The wallet has a customizable interface. However, the only drawback is that it is an online wallet and should not be used to store a large amount of money.

Another desktop wallet you can use is the Jaxx wallet. It was developed by Anthony Diiorio, Ethereum co-founder. It is compatible with Windows, Mac, and Android. You can use it across multiple devices. It stores Bitcoin, Ethereum, Zcash, and others.

Mobile

This is a mobile wallet that you can download and install on your phone. A mobile wallet is not different from your traditional wallet. You can travel with it and make purchases on the go. Mobile wallets are slightly risky as it is easy to lose your smartphone.

Online wallets

Online wallets are programs that store your wealth online. You can access the wallets using any device connected to the internet. This gives you convenience but poses a great security risk. Online wallets can also include exchanges. It is always a good idea to store only a small portion of your money in online wallets.

A good example of an online wallet is the Bitpanda wallet. You can use the wallet to buy, sell, and store several coins such as Bitcoin, Ripple, Dash, Litecoin, Ethereum, and Bitcoin Cash. The wallet is free to use. It has a simple user interface that will get you going in no time.

Hardware

This is the kind of wallet you should have when you own a lot of cryptocurrencies. Hardware wallets are hardware devices solely dedicated to storing your crypto wealth. It is very secure as your wallet is stored offline.

The Ledger/Trezor wallet is among the top hardware wallets you can buy. It allows you to store Bitcoin, Ripple, Stellar, Litecoin, and several other coins. It has a built-in display screen that allows you to see and confirm transactions. You can also connect it to a computer via a USB connection. It is secure and allows you to recover your money in case you lose your wallet.

Paper

A paper wallet keeps the copy of your private keys on paper. You can then store the paper in a secure place such as a safe. A paper wallet can have a barcode that you scan. This will allow you to send and receive money. A paper wallet is a secure wallet option as it keeps your private keys away from the public domain.

The Cryo Card wallet is a good paper wallet that can secure your money in cold storage. The wallet has the shape and feel of credit/debit card. It is made of stainless steel. It is secure and can withstand fire, floods, acids, bases, temperatures, and salt water. It supports Bitcoin.

Before investing

Cryptocurrencies would not have attracted so much attention if they did not allow people to invest in them and reap 'real' rewards. I call them real rewards because some investors have made north of 1,000% in investment returns. I am sure you are familiar with such stories. Bitcoin started without any value nor any promise of it.

In time, people caught the Bitcoin fever and nine years later, we are where we are today. 1 Bitcoin is almost worth $10,000. That is a lot. There is even speculation and expectation for it to go even higher. Some analysts have suggested that it may reach as high as $100,000 in the next few years. Nothing is impossible with Bitcoin.

This is the reason why many people invest in it. And we wouldn't be surprised if you want to.

Big disclaimer:

You will get a marathon journey about investing in Bitcoin or Ripple. However, I have to make it clear from the onset that I am not a financial advisor. I am not a Wall Street expert. I have learned over the years that the investment world is not generous and fair at all. The information you find in this book is not professional advice. Do not rely on it to make investments. However, you can use it in conjunction with your own research and due diligence.

Let's immediately dive into the world of crypto investments.

Investment mindset

Investing is not an activity that you can engage in without the right frame of mind. Even the most successful investors such as Warren Buffet, Paul Tudor Jones, George Soros, etc. do not just invest anyhow. They first need to get the right investment mindset. This is the mindset that I am going to be writing about. The mindset of a winning investor.

You first need to understand that you are an investor and not a gambler. So, what's the difference between the two? Approach and attitude.

A gambler thrives and survives on luck. An investor survives on informed decisions. Your first priority as an investor is to get as much as information before you make a decision. There is nothing like a safe investment. Every investment activity involves some risk and the potential to lose some or all of your money. An intelligent and successful investor takes calculated risks.

"Until you can manage your mind, do not expect to manage money."
Warren Buffet

What kind of a mindset do you then need in order to become a successful investor?

Commitment

Needless to say, there are a few things that can be achieved without commitment. The first you need is a commitment to your investment career or part-time activity. This is not something you should partake after a disappointing day at work or when you have had a fight with your loved ones.

You need to approach this seriously. This means that you need to do all the necessary and sometimes dirty work of researching what you want to research in. Tell yourself that you are in for the long term. Always remember your end goal. This will always push you to stay in the game even when there is no reason to.

It becomes more important when it comes to investing in cryptocurrencies. Cryptocurrencies are highly volatile. They need people with a steady mind and are not easily moved by market changes.

Keep your emotions in check

Emotions are the biggest downfall of the majority of traders and investors. Do not attach yourself to a particular coin or token. Only invest in a coin that is worth investing in.

Know when to exit and when to continue in the game. Be strong enough to stick to your game plan. The truth is that things will not always go your way. There are times when you will lose your investments. It has happened to thousands of people and it might happen to you. However, that should not control you or instill fear in you.

If an investment is not going your way, decide if you should exit or hold for some time. Be sure to keep your emotions out of an investment decision you make.

Do not invest in new tokens/coins simply because your previous investment did not go well. This quick desire to "fix things" can only lead to more damage. Instead, take your time to study what went wrong. Give your emotions time to cool down. Emotional decisions are not always the best logical ones. Investing requires logic and not emotions.

Cryptocurrencies

Have a solid strategy

It is one thing to have a good idea and it is another to execute that idea brilliantly. There are so many coins/tokens that you invest or trade.

How then do you hedge yourself against losing your investment?

You need to be observant before you start investing or picking out your perceived digital winners. Develop a hypothesis on how to pick your winners. Test it if possible and if time allows.

Cryptocurrencies have played their part in minting new and unexpected millionaires. It can do the same for you. This does not come easily though. You need to know how to spot the winning opportunities.

Only go investments or trades that offer you decent returns with minimum risk. The market is already risky. There is no need to add more risk to it.

This is a country road. It will get dusty and nasty. You should be prepared for that beforehand. Take risks where possible.

You will make mistakes

No one wants to hear this but you have to hear it. You are not a machine. You will make mistakes at some point. This is unavoidable. What is avoidable is repeating the same mistake over and over again.

"The greatest mistake you will ever make is making the same mistake twice."

Whenever you make a mistake, acknowledge it. Write it down. Mistakes take you on a path of discovery. Learn and grow from them. You can never know it all if you are an investor. You are on a path of discovery and making money.

Be your own person

The one-size-fits-all rule does not apply to all investors. Each one has his/her own signature investment/trading philosophy. You need to have your own.

Do not ride the train that others ride. Be prepared to walk in the desert if you have to. Do not be afraid of being uncomfortable if you have to.

Only associate yourself with people who share the same vision as you. Avoid being around people who instill negative thoughts in you.

You can only be you if you associate with people who allow you to be your own kind of investor. Learn from your mistakes. Experience is the biggest teacher. Learn from it. Let is shape you as an investor.

Be a unique investor/trader. You do not have to be ashamed of it.

Be passionate

Many people invest for the sole purpose of making money. There is nothing wrong with this. We all need money to survive.

Investing is not a stroll in the park. You may lose money along the way. You will likely lose some of your money too.

You will quit at the first hurdle if you are not prepared for this.

You have to be passionate about investing. This is what will keep you going when things are not going your way. Passion takes beyond the wall that stops the majority from crossing over to the other side.

Passion will stop you from quitting. Passion and discipline are what you need to be successful.

Putting it all together

These are not the ten commandments of the mindset of an investor. They are the guidelines that will help you find your true self in the investment world. Put these traits to use. Keep on searching who you are.

You can only find success when you find your true space in the universe. You are a star. Find your position in the sky and you will be able to give some light to the world.

Your light is your success as an investor.

Paper profits vs. actual profits

Your main aim as an investor is to make profits. You are not that different from someone who is running a business. You are similar in the sense that you put your capital on the line, carry out an activity with the hope of realizing a profit.

Business profits/losses are different from investment profits/losses. I will constantly refer to profit because our collective aim is to make huge profits. Who wants to lose anywhere?

As an investor, you buy your stock or cryptocurrency and hold it in your investment portfolio. The next thing you do is track its price changes. If its prices become higher than the prices you bought it for, you have made a profit. However, you cannot access the profit yet or use it. A profit only exists on paper.

This profit is not yet secure. It can change anytime. It can go up or down. It signifies that you are still in the game. In addition, being in the game means that you are exposed to more profits or running a loss. You cannot spend this profit.

In simple terms, its profit you have but do not own yet. However, it is entirely up to you to decide when you want to cash out.

The moment you decide to cash out is the moment you have actual profit. This is the profit you actually have and use as you wish. I like to call it the hard profit because it is tangible, usable, and distributable.

There is a bad side to paper profits. They can make you a theoretical billionaire/millionaire but in reality, you may even struggle to pay your bills. Some rules and clauses in your stock/option contract may prevent you from liquidating your investment until a certain time. You may even lose your paper profit before you realize it. The dot-com boom produced poor "paper millionaires". This is because they held stocks and securities that were profitable. However, the law prevented them to sell the stock in their portfolio until a certain date. The dotcom bubble popped and the theoretical millionaires were back at square one.

There are also paper losses. They are not different from paper profits except that you are in the red. The bone of contention is what you should do with paper losses. Some people argue that you should hold them with the hope that they will turn into profits. This is a good idea but risky as well. Your losses may sink deeper.

A successful investor should know how to deal with losses as much he/she knows how to deal with profits. There are times when it makes more sense to cash out your paper losses and turn them into actual losses.

For the record, I hate losses of any kind. There are times when they are unavoidable. This critical situation requires quick thinking and great decision-making. Let us take a look at some of the moments when it makes sense to realize your paper losses rather than holding them.

Avoid further losses

Cashing out early on will prevent you from incurring further losses as the price of the stocks or crypto coin. Some coins are frauds. Many of them are defunct. It is better to salvage a portion of your investment capital than to walk away empty-handed.

Have more cash

If your coin continues on a downward trend and you are assured that it may not turn things around, cash out and have more money to diversify your portfolio.

Sharpen your thinking

Going through some losses will sharpen your thinking. It will cause you not to blindly invest in any coin or stock without conducting due diligence. If you did your part to the latter and the coin still resulted in you registering a loss, all you have to do is walk away while you can. Sharpen your mind while you wait for the next coin to invest in.

A paper loss is an elephant in the room

A paper loss affects your thinking. The pain you feel reduces your productivity and might affect your ability to make profitable investments in the future. Taking it out of the picture may give cause to see things differently. You will not have anything to weigh you down.

Special note on cryptocurrencies

Cryptocurrencies are highly volatile. This is a basic rule you must know when investing in them. Paper losses should not put you in panic mode when you have invested in cryptocurrencies. Be patient. The prices may adjust themselves and you end up on a winning.

Do not be quick to cash out on paper losses.

Long-term investing vs. day trading

Think of investing and day trading as two different routes that lead you to the same destination. The common goal of investing or trading is to accumulate wealth through buying stocks, crypto coins/tokens, etc. and holding them for a certain period until they appreciate in value. The only difference between the two is how long you hold the coins/tokens in your portfolio until you sell.

The million dollar question is probably which one is better between the two.

The actual answer depends on a number of factors. I will simply list the pros and cons of each and you will decide for yourself which one is better. Sometimes, you have to make your own choices depending on the available information. What works for Jane does not necessarily have to work for John.

Investing

Investing in cryptocurrencies is known as HODLing. The investors are known as HODLers. HODL simply stands for Hold On for Dear Life. Investing allows to have a portfolio of tokens/coins and hold them for a long time. The holding period allows you to earn profits.

Here are the pros of investing or HODLing:

- You are not affected by the daily fluctuations of the market – cryptocurrencies are very volatile. HODLing gives you peace of mind as your aim is to make profits in the long run.

- HODLing can be profitable even for first-time investors. All they have to do is buy, hold, and cash out when the markets are attractive.

- No emotions. Longtime investments automatically keep your emotions in check. You do not need to check the market movements on a daily basis (though some do that). Any decline in the market is not likely going to affect you.

- Effortless. You don't need to put a lot of effort as compared to day trading. It also does not require much time commitment as compared to day trading. However, you still need to do your due diligence before investing to make sure that you are picking coins/tokens that will be profitable in the long run.

Here are the few cons of investing

- You may miss out on daily market jumps

Day trading

Day trading is not for the faint of heart. Here are some pros for crypto day trading.

- Compounding. You can quickly grow your investment capital by pouring in your profits for today in tomorrow's trades.

- You can make an instant profit from daily market movements.

Its cons are as follows:

- Not suitable for beginners as it carries many risks. It can result in the complete loss of your investment capital in a short space of time.

- Requires more time per day. You have to dedicate a portion of daily time to trading.

- Involves a lot of emotions due to market movements that happen each day.

- You may be trading against bots and machines. The odds won't be in your favor.

- The attention and hard work required may add some stress to your life.

- High transaction fees. A chunk of your investment and profit is swallowed in transaction fees due to the several trades and transactions you carry out on a single day.

Investment/trading techniques

There are several techniques you can use in your investment/trading strategy. However, it is important that you understand each technique so that you can use it to your advantage. I have listed a few techniques below.

Fundamental analysis

Fundamental analysis is simply the application of economics, investor sentiment, and current events to determine the price or future price of the crypto markets.

The fundamental analysis of cryptocurrencies is totally different from the fundamental analysis of public companies. This is because of the differences between cryptocurrencies and public companies. Moreover, the crypto market is still young and there is a long way to go in analyzing crypto tokens/tokens. Fortunately, there are some ways that you can use to determine if a token/coin is worth investing in. These include:

- Token/coin value or utility
- News and publicity

I will now go over each of the points above in detail.

Value or utility

A good coin/token must do something unique. It should solve a problem. This is one easy way to see if a coin/token will still be useful in the next five or ten years.

Ask yourself this question, what does the question do? You can get this answer from reading and analyzing their white paper. The white paper should be fairly technical without any sort of marketing or fake promises.

If you can ascertain that a coin can solve a problem, then it may be worth looking at. You also need to consider the people behind the currency. This includes both the technical and executive team.

You then need to consider the coin's roadmap. Check what the coin initially aimed to achieve and what they have achieved so far. This can be easily interpreted by looking at how much they raised in the ICO and how they spent it.

If at some point you feel that the coin/token may be a scam, then it may be one. A real project does not many red flags if it does at all. Fundamental analysis is all about checking if a coin has one or more red flags. Stay away from those coins.

News and publicity

Avoid any coin/tokens that are associated with bad publicity. A good project should be in the news for the right reasons.

A good project must be in the news for its progress. It must be mentioned for its worthiness and how it can contribute significantly to solving problems.

Technical analysis

Technical analysis is an investing/trading technique that forecasts future market prices based on historical data such as prices, trading volume, market cap, etc. Technical analysis is mainly used by day traders.

The technical analysis predicts the future using past data. The most important aspect of this technique is to pick up trends and make decisions based on those trends. Technical analysts use bar charts, candlesticks, and statistics to make their decisions.

Averaging down

There are times when you buy a coin and suddenly it drops its price. This is the case if you have been following the crypto market lately. Some investors employ the "averaging down" technique as a way to minimize the potential loss and maybe even make a profit.

The best way to understand averaging down is to illustrate it by means of simple mathematics. Let's assume that you decide to buy coin XYZ at a price of $5/coin. You pay $500 for 100 coins. The price falls to $2.50 shortly after. In theory, you have made a paper loss of 50%.

This prompts you to buy more shares at the low rate. You buy extra

100 shares at $250. Together, you have bought 200 coins at $750. The new average price of the coin is $3.75. If the coin picks up and makes it to $4, then you have made an "average profit" on all your 200 coins. You can sell them for $800 leaving you with a profit of $50.00.

Is averaging down a good strategy? Yes and no is the answer.

There are several factors that necessitate a price drop. The coin may not increase in the short term. The price may even fall down further. This will leave you with further losses. Averaging down also allows your "bruised ego" to sink you deeper. It may seem like a way out but actually, it's a way to take away more money from you.

On the other hand, averaging down may lead to a price increase. Even if the coin does not make it past $5 (your initial investment), you still make a profit.

All in all, you need to be careful before you think of averaging down. It may be a good strategy since the crypto market is very volatile.

Pump and dump strategies

Tokens are not created equal. Not all creators of cryptocurrencies can be trusted. Some just want to cash on the hype. The cold and harsh truth is that there are scams out there. It is your duty to recognize or smell them from afar and stay as far away as possible.

Some creators develop a coin and keep as many coins as possible for them. This basically gives them the power to control the market and even crash it if they want to. They will hold their substantial stake while they create some hype around the coin.

When the coin fetches a higher price, they can sell all their coins. This floods and crashes the market. Such a strategy is known as a pump and dump scheme.

The good news is that you can avoid it. You have to analyze the coin and find out the portion reserved for the development team. Be careful of projects where the development team control a substantial amount of the coins/tokens. It sort of centralizes the currency and gives them the power to crash if they want to.

Governmental measures and policies on cryptocurrencies

We all knew that it was a matter of time before governments began to notice the attention that cryptocurrencies are getting and do something about it. Governments do something by passing laws and adopting new policies that either promote or prohibit the new tech in question.

Cryptocurrencies seem to have been on the radar of some influential countries in the past few months. This came off the back of Bitcoin trading as high as $19,000+ in December 2017. It could be one of the factors that triggered some governments to act.

China was the main actor. It cracked down on Bitcoin exchanges citing the currencies to be illegal. This also spiraled to other countries such as South Korea. South Korea took a similar stance as China. The Indian government has indicated that there is a need for the cryptocurrency market to be regulated.

The regulation itself may not be a bad idea. Some are in favor of it because they believe that there are scam ICOs that are conning people their money. A government intervention would solve this.

Another section of cryptocurrency users claims that governments are trying to take control of cryptocurrencies the same way they control fiat money. This does not sit well with them.

There are also some countries like Venezuela that have gone to the extent of creating their own digital currencies. Venezuela recently launched the Petro token which is backed by oil and gas. This has sparked some controversy from within the borders of the country. The main political opposition party is accusing the government of creating the digital currency in order to cover up its mess.

Internationally, some countries are not endorsing the move as they believe that it allows Venezuela to circumvent sanctions imposed on it. Some countries are considering having their own cryptocurrencies. These include China and Iran.

The truth is that there is a long way to go before governments can fully enact policies that will either monitor or ban cryptocurrencies altogether. In the meantime, cryptocurrencies have a promising future and may even be legal tender in several countries in the next few years.

Putting it altogether

Be warned that investing in cryptocurrencies carries high risk and be cautious. I encourage you not to invest blindly. You have to do your due diligence before putting your money away. The crypto market is young and volatile. You can make huge profits or easily lose all your life savings.

You can minimize the risk by following an investment protocol. This involves doing thorough research in as many coins as possible. You then narrow it down to a few potential winners. Invest in a diverse number of coins.

Never put all your eggs in one basket.

Lastly, only invest money that you can afford to lose. Do not invest your entire salary or money that you need for paying your bills. That money can be wiped away in an instant. Lastly, be in the right frame of mind before you start investing. Learn to control your emotions. Investing, if not done properly, can ruin you the same way that gambling has ruined several people.

On the bright side, investing or trading cryptocurrencies has produced millionaires. You can be the next millionaire. Avoid being counted among losers.

JOHAN VON AMSTERDAM

Who is the winner, Bitcoin or Ripple?

It is common that many people ask which one is the better token/coin between Bitcoin and Ripple. Let's briefly take a look at each coin and what purpose it serves.

I will start off with Bitcoin, the big brother. Bitcoin is considered to be a "store of value." This, in a certain way, puts on the same par as fiat currency. This is not surprising because it has already been called the "digital gold." It has some similarities to gold. It can be used as a currency. Many people are now aware of it and its potential.

Some big institutions such as central banks and governments are afraid of it. They ought to be. Bitcoin is slowly changing the way we send, receive, and store money. Central banks are known for being the custodians of fiat money and Bitcoin is particularly threatening their own existence.

This obviously will not sit well with them. They will try to monitor it and regulate it in order to stop it from becoming a mainstream currency.

On the other hand, Ripple seems to be doing well in forming partnerships with banks. The Ripple protocol was specifically designed for banks. There is a general argument that it is partially centralized. Ripple and Bitcoin are fundamentally different. Bitcoin is a currency while Ripple is a utility token. It is then difficult to compare the two. More importantly, they are not in direct completion. In fact, Ripple complements Bitcoin. These two are meant to co-exist together in the financial ecosystem.

Cryptocurrencies

There is no winner between Ripple and Bitcoin. They both serve their purpose well.

JOHAN VON AMSTERDAM

Thank you!

A gift as a thank you!

The cryptocurrency world is a fast moving world. Knowledge is power and the world of the cryptocurrencies keeps evolving.

If you want to stay up-to-date, please check out the author's website:

www.aboutcryptocurrencies.net.

Here you will find the latest cryptocurrencies news gathered from around the world and updated multiple times per day. Sign-up for the 'Daily Crypto News' and receive the electronic version of the officially published book: 'Bitcoin: What is Bitcoin?' for free as a thank you for buying this book.

So go to www.aboutcryptocurrencies.net, sign up and get the ebook for free as a thank you.

Finally, if you enjoyed this book, then I'd like to ask you for a favor, would you be kind enough to leave a review for this book on Amazon? It'd be greatly appreciated!

Thank you for reading and I want to wish you the best in the world of cryptocurrencies.

Yours sincerely,

Johan von Amsterdam

www.ingramcontent.com/pod-product-compliance
Lightning Source LLC
Chambersburg PA
CBHW020650220526
45464CB00001B/369